MAN ASKS,
GOD ANSWERS

D1013593

CRAIG R. BROWN

craigbrown0530 @gmail.com
3326 Marsden Pt.
Keswick, VA 22947

Cover design by: Dual Identity, Inc.
Interior design and typeset: Katherine Lloyd, The DESK

To contact the author, email CraigBrown0530@gmail.com.

Library of Congress Cataloging-in-Publication Data

Brown, Craig R., 1956-
  Man asks God answers / Craig R. Brown.
    pages cm
  Includes bibliographical references.
  ISBN 978-0-615-65704-2
1. Theology, Doctrinal. 2. Reformed Church--Doctrines. I. Title.

  BT75.3.B76 2012
  230'.42--dc23

2012026263

Contents

THE ANSWERS TO SEVEN OF LIFE'S TOUGHEST QUESTIONS

Man is naturally inquisitive. Throughout history, thinking human beings have wanted to know the answers to life's toughest questions: Who am I? Why am I here? Where do I go from here? This book is an attempt to provide the answers to seven of these questions that have intrigued mankind. It is written in a simple, readable format for the person who wants to know the truth.

We exist in a world where many people believe that each person can find his "own truth" and then convince himself that he is correct. This subjective way of looking at life presumes that man can figure it all out for himself and that there may be many "truths," depending on one's personal perspective or background. This book begins with the assumption that there is one absolute truth, and it is our responsibility to do everything we can to find it.

In the same way, there are two ways of investigating the truth in this life. We can base our thinking on what we each conclude for ourselves using our own reasoning or we can base it on what God says. If you, like most people, are struggling to find the truth, please take the time to read this book. Hopefully, after reading it, you will see the fallacy in the former method of seeking the truth and the joy in the latter.

Man Asks, God Answers is not meant to be a complete discussion of these seven questions. It is meant to be a thought-provoking introduction to each question, with the challenge to read more on these topics and suggested resources to do so.

My prayer is that this book will lead you to an understanding of the truth and a desire to fall on your knees and thank God for His undisputed love and sovereignty over your life and this world.

Chapter 1

IS THERE A GOD
AND IS HE IN CONTROL?

Where do you start in seeking an answer to the question, "Is there a God?" Throughout most of history, the existence of a god or gods has been an accepted belief. Almost every culture, from ancient Greece and Rome to those of the Far East and pre-Columbian America, had a belief in a divine authority or creator of some type. Only in modern times has man begun to question whether God actually exists. With the development of the theory of evolution by Charles Darwin in the mid-1800s, man, for the first time, had a way of explaining the formation of life without the need for a divine creator.

In the twenty-first century, the question we must confront is whether any thinking, reasoning, intelligent human being can look at the complexities of the world in which we live—from the human body to mathematics to nuclear fission to the beauty of nature—and possibly believe all this happened by chance from the ooze of non-life. Is it not logical to believe that something at least set everything in motion and was the initial cause of everything that exists? Modern science embraces the "big bang" theory of the formation of the universe, but most scientists now believe that some force had to initiate the big bang.

God tells us that it was *Him*. In Genesis 1:3, 6, 9, 11, 14, 20, and 24, the Bible says that "God said" and the heavens, earth, light, oceans, sun, moon, stars, and all living creatures were created. Whether this took six days, six "periods of time," or six seconds, while important, does not matter when discussing the "who did it" question. God says He created it, and we have absolutely no reason not to believe Him.

He then tells us that in order to know He exists, we need only to look at what He created. Romans 1:20 explains: "For his invisible attributes, namely, his eternal power and divine nature, have been clearly perceived, ever since the creation of the world, in the things that have been made. So they are without excuse." Here, the apostle Paul, the writer to the Roman church in the New Testament, is saying that there is more than enough evidence in nature alone to prove the existence of a God who created the world. Look at the animals, the trees, the flowers. It is simply logical to see the need for a divine being to create these fabulously detailed and beautiful organisms. In other words, the Bible says this is "common sense."

So, in answer to the first part of our first question, "Is there a God?" God says, "Yes—can't you tell by My creation?"

Who Is in Control?

If we are willing to concede that there is a God, the next part of our first question is this: "Does it matter?" In other words, is God in control of the world that He created or is man in control? It appears that these are the only two options. Is God sovereign (in charge of, ruling over) in His creation or is man responsible for his actions? How you answer this question determines what kind of god you believe in.

The truth is that both options are true. God is sovereign (He has predetermined everything from the foundation of the world) and man is responsible (we make our own decisions and are not puppets of anyone).

These twin truths seem totally irreconcilable. If God has predetermined everything that happens, how can our decisions mean anything? Since we make decisions, how can God be sovereign? We must go to Scripture to find the resolution to this apparent contradiction. We'll start with Exodus.

During the account of the plagues that God brought upon Egypt, the Bible repeatedly says that Pharaoh hardened his heart and refused to let his Israelite slaves go (Ex.

7:13, 14, 22; 8:15). In other words, Pharaoh chose to disobey God of his own free will. However, the Lord had planned it that way, which is why the Bible also says God hardened Pharaoh's heart (Ex. 4:21; 7:3; 9:12).

At first glance, this doesn't make sense. But the Bible tells us in at least two other places that God controls the leaders of nations. Proverbs 21:1 says, "The king's heart is a stream of water in the hand of the LORD; he turns it wherever he will." And Daniel 2:20–21 says: "Blessed be the name of God forever and ever, to whom belong wisdom and might. He changes times and seasons; he removes kings and sets up kings; he gives wisdom to the wise and knowledge to those who have understanding."

But God's control of kings is just one aspect of His authority. He is sovereign over His universe. He determines everything that happens, both to kings and to you and me. Consider these verses that speak of God's sovereignty:

"I know that you can do all things, and that no purpose of yours can be thwarted." (Job 42:2)

The Lord has established his throne in the heavens, and his kingdom rules over all. (Ps. 103:19)

In your book were written, every one of them, the days that were formed for me, when as yet there were none of them. (Ps. 139:16b) (This verse is somewhat difficult to understand, but it is simply saying that God knew and determined every day of your life prior to your birth.)

The LORD of hosts has sworn: "As I have planned, so shall it be, and as I have purposed, so shall it stand." (Isa. 14:24)

"I am God, and there is none like me, declaring the end from the beginning and from ancient times things not yet done, saying, 'My counsel shall stand, and I will accomplish all my purpose.'" (Isa. 46:9b–10)

"So shall my word be that goes out from my mouth; it shall not return to me empty, but it shall accomplish that which I purpose, and shall succeed in the thing for which I sent it." (Isa. 55:11)

For by grace you have been saved through faith. And this is not your own doing; it is the gift of God, not a result of works, so that no one may boast. (Eph. 2:8–9)

God's Will and Man's Will

Clearly, then, Scripture shows that God is sovereign. But we all know we have free will. If you decide right now to shut this book because you do not like what you are reading, you will do so of your own free will. No one will force you to do it. Yet if you do it, it will be because God predetermined that you would. How can this be?

Wayne Grudem explains this dual truth as the doctrine of concurrence. He defines it this way: "The fact that God cooperates with created things in every action, directing their distinctive properties to cause them to act as they do."[1]

With this understanding, it is possible to affirm that, in every event, both God's sovereign will and man's will are active. God brings His will to pass, not by canceling the will of the creature, but by working through the will of the creature. God's will is the "primary cause"; He works behind the scenes from the beginning of time to plan and initiate everything that happens. Man's will is the "secondary cause"; it carries out events in a manner consistent with God's will.

For example, when God wishes to save a sinner, He does not strike the individual with "divine lightning." Rather, He uses a godly man to witness to that individual. Man, the "secondary cause," appears to be the only cause, but in reality, God is the "primary cause," for He works in the evangelist's heart to give him the desire to witness and in the recipient's heart to allow him to accept the truth he is receiving.

The fact of God's providential direction as an unseen, behind-the-scenes "primary cause" should not lead us to deny the reality of our choices and actions. Again and again Scripture affirms that we really do cause events to happen.

We are significant and we are responsible. We have choices, real choices that bring about real results. The following Scripture verses demonstrate man's responsibility and choice:

Tell the righteous that it shall be well with them, for they shall eat the fruit of their deeds. (Isa. 3:10)

"Again, when a wicked person turns away from the wickedness he has committed and does what is just and right, he shall save his life. Because he considered and turned away from all the transgressions that he had committed, he shall surely live; he shall not die." (Ezek. 18:27–28)

"When the righteous turns from his righteousness and does injustice, he shall die for it. And when the wicked turns from his wickedness and does what is just and right, he shall live by this." (Ezek. 33:18–19)

"The one who endures to the end will be saved." (Matt. 24:13)

"Whoever believes in him is not condemned, but whoever does not believe is condemned already, because he has not believed in the name of the only Son of God." (John 3:18)

"Whoever hears my word and believes him who sent me has eternal life. He does not come into judgment, but has passed from death to life." (John 5:24)

"The one who rejects me and does not receive my words has a judge; the word that I have spoken will judge him on the last day." (John 12:48)

"Repent and be baptized every one of you in the name of Jesus Christ for the forgiveness of your sins, and you will receive the gift of the Holy Spirit." (Acts 2:38)

He will render to each one according to his works: to those who by patience in well-doing seek for glory and honor and immortality, he will give eternal life; but for those who are self-seeking and do not obey the truth, but obey unrighteousness, there will be wrath and fury. (Rom. 2:6–8)

Let not sin therefore reign in your mortal body, to make you obey its passions. (Rom. 6:12)

If you confess with your mouth that Jesus is Lord and believe in your heart that God raised him from the dead, you will be saved. (Rom. 10:9)

The fruit of the Spirit is love, joy, peace, patience, kindness, goodness, faithfulness, gentleness, self-control. (Gal. 5:22–23a)

So then, brothers, stand firm and hold to the traditions that you were taught by us. (2 Thess. 2:15a)

Understanding the Mystery

God causes all things that happen, but He does so in such a way that He somehow upholds our ability to make willing, responsible choices that have real and eternal results, and for which we are held accountable. Exactly how God combines His providential control with our willing and significant choices, Scripture does not explain to us. But rather than deny one aspect or the other simply because we cannot explain how both can be true, we should accept both in an attempt to be faithful to the teaching of all of Scripture.[2]

One of the clearest examples of concurrence in Scripture occurs in the story of Jonah. Jonah was an Old Testament prophet whom God sent to preach to the city of Nineveh. Rather than obey God in this task, Jonah ran away. In his flight from God, Jonah was on a ship. God caused a storm to develop, and the crew blamed it on Jonah. The author of this biblical book tells us that the men on the ship threw Jonah into the sea and simultaneously affirms that it was God who threw him overboard (see Jonah 1:15; 2:3). God's providential direction of events did not coerce the sailors to act against their wills. They were unaware that He was influencing their behavior and they actually prayed for His forgiveness. God chose to act through the choices of these real human beings, men who were morally account-able for their actions, in order to bring about His plan for the salvation of Nineveh. He caused them to choose to do what they did, but they did it willingly, with no knowledge of His influence. God did not cause them to sin; they did exactly what their hearts wanted to do, but it was within God's sovereign purpose.

To reinforce the truth that the Bible teaches both God's sovereignty and man's responsibility, I want to look at three additional verses that talk about both doctrines.

Proverbs 16:9 says, "The heart of man plans his way, but the Lord establishes his steps." Here God affirms that we human beings plan out our lives and make our deci-sions, but He already has determined what will occur.

Proverbs 19:21 reads, "Many are the plans in the mind of a man, but it is the purpose of the Lord that will stand." Here God again says that man makes his plans according to his own desires, but those plans are perfectly matched with God's purposes.

Finally, in John 6:37, Jesus says, "All that the Father gives me will come to me, and whoever comes to me I will never cast out." This is my favorite verse in the Bible, because in it we see the dual truths of God's election of His people and the freedom for anyone who so desires to come to Him and be one of His.

"All that the Father gives me" refers to those individuals

whom God has chosen from the foundation of the world to believe in Him. "Will come to me" means that, some time in their lives, those individuals will choose to believe in Christ as their Savior and their Lord. "And whoever comes to me" means that the invitation is open to anyone to believe in Christ. "I will never cast out" means that anyone who does come to Christ will be saved.

In this one verse we see the twin truths of God's sovereignty and man's responsibility side by side. How can God have planned all events yet man still be responsible for his actions? This does not appear to make logical sense. How can it be true? Can we be bold enough to question God on this apparent contradiction? God knows this question is on our minds, and He gives us a fabulous passage that answers this question. In Romans 9:14–24, which I believe to be the most powerful passage in the Bible, we read:

> What shall we say then? Is there injustice on God's part? By no means! For he says to Moses, "I will have mercy on whom I have mercy, and I will have compassion on whom I have compassion." So then it depends not on human will or exertion, but on God, who has mercy. For the Scripture says to Pharaoh, "For this very purpose I have raised you up, that I might show my power in you, and that my name might be proclaimed in all the earth." So

then he has mercy on whomever he wills, and he hardens whomever he wills.

You will say to me then, "Why does he still find fault? For who can resist his will?" But who are you, O man, to answer back to God? Will what is molded say to its molder, "Why have you made me like this?" Has the potter no right over the clay, to make out of the same lump one vessel for honored use and another for dishonorable use? What if God, desiring to show his wrath and to make known his power, has endured with much patience vessels of wrath prepared for destruction, in order to make known the riches of his glory for vessels of mercy, which he has prepared beforehand for glory—even us whom he has called, not from the Jews only but also from the Gentiles?

In Paul's hypothetical example, man is questioning God's fairness. God's basic response is this: "Who do you think you are? I am God. You are man. There is a big difference."

So the answer to the question of how God can harden Pharaoh's heart and Pharaoh can yet make his own decisions is simple—God set it up that way. He is God, so He can do anything He wants. Just because our finite minds cannot comprehend something He does has no effect on the reality of it.

While we are free from our perspective, we must realize that absolute "freedom"—total freedom from God's control—is simply not possible in a world providentially sustained and directed by God Himself. Human freedom is real, but it is everywhere limited by God's freedom. God is sovereign, not man. His sovereignty is never limited by human freedom. Rather, human freedom is always limited by God's sovereignty.

The simple fact of the matter is that no event falls outside of God's providence; if it did, He would not be God. Because Paul knew that God is sovereign over all and works His purposes in every event that happens, he could declare that "for those who love God all things work together for good, for those who are called according to his purpose" (Rom. 8:28).

Meditate on these additional verses on God's sovereignty and love for his people:

Therefore David blessed the LORD in the presence of all the assembly. And David said: "Blessed are you, O LORD, the God of Israel our father, forever and ever. Yours, O LORD, is the greatness and the power and the glory and the victory and the majesty, for all that is in the heavens and in the earth is yours. Yours is the kingdom, O LORD, and you are exalted as head above all. Both riches and honor come from you, and you rule over all. In your hand are power and might, and in your hand it is to make great and to give strength to all." (1 Chron. 29:10–12)

Then Job answered the LORD and said: "I know that you can do all things, and that no purpose of yours can be thwarted." (Job 42:1–2)

Our God is in the heavens; he does all that he pleases. (Ps. 115:3)

Whatever the LORD pleases, he does, in heaven and on earth, in the seas and all deeps. (Ps. 135:6)

The LORD of hosts has sworn: "As I have planned, so shall it be, and as I have purposed, so shall it stand. . . ." For the LORD of hosts has purposed, and who will annul it? His hand is stretched out, and who will turn it back? (Isa. 14:24–27)

"Ah, Lord GOD! It is you who has made the heavens and the earth by your great power and by your outstretched arm! Nothing is too hard for you." (Jer. 32:17)

All the inhabitants of the earth are accounted as nothing, and he does according to his will among the host of heaven and among the inhabitants of the earth. (Dan. 4:35a)

"Then the King will say to those on his right, 'Come, you who are blessed by my Father, inherit the kingdom prepared for you from the foundation of the world.'" (Matt. 25:34)

"No one can come to me unless the Father who sent me draws him." (John 6:44a)

"You did not choose me, but I chose you and appointed you that you should go and bear fruit." (John 15:16a)

"And he made from one man every nation of mankind to live on all the face of the earth, having determined allotted periods and the boundaries of their dwelling place." (Acts 17:26)

For those whom he foreknew he also predestined to be conformed to the image of his Son, in order that he might be the firstborn among many brothers. And those whom he predestined he also called, and those whom he called he also justified, and those whom he justified he also glorified. (Rom. 8:29–30)

He chose us in him before the foundation of the world, that we should be holy and blameless before him. In love he predestined us for adoption as sons through Jesus Christ, according to the purpose of his will. (Eph. 1:4–5)

God chose you as the firstfruits to be saved, through sanctification by the Spirit and belief in the truth. (2 Thess. 2:13b)

These last three passages use a number of terms that may not be familiar to you. Here are quick explanations that will aid your understanding:

• "Foreknew"—To foreknow is to know something before it happens. God's foreknowledge is infinite. It speaks of a predetermined choice to set His love on us and establish an intimate relationship with us.

• "Predestined"—To predestine is to mark out, appoint, or determine beforehand. The eternal, sovereign, immutable, and unconditional decrees of God govern all events.

• "Firstborn"—The firstborn son is the preeminent one, the one who is the only rightful heir.

• "Called"—God's call is His act of drawing to Himself all those He has chosen for salvation. God has set believers apart from sin unto Himself, so they are holy ones.

- "Justified"—To justify a person is to declare him righteous. Pardon from the guilt and penalty of sin, and the imputation of Christ's righteousness to the believer's account, make him acceptable to God.
- "Glorified"—Glorification is the eternal security of all those who are saved to live forever with God in the new heaven and new earth.
- "Adoption"—Adoption is the process of becoming a child of God. Man receives not only Christ's blessings but also His very nature.
- "Sanctification"—Sanctification is the work of the Holy Spirit to bring the nature of man into conformity to God's will. It is the perfecting of the work done in regeneration, and it brings the believer into an understanding of the truth. It is a lifelong process.

Because He is both God and man, Jesus knows the dual truth of God's sovereignty and man's responsibility from both perspectives. The Bible teaches us that God sent His own Son, Jesus, to earth to live the perfect life for us and to pay the penalty for our sins. On the night before His crucifixion (death on the cross), He prayed: "Father, if you are willing, remove this cup from me. Nevertheless, not my will, but yours, be done" (Luke 22:42). God had predestined all the actions of all the participants in Jesus' crucifixion. Yet the apostles never blame God for the actions that resulted from the willing choices of sinful men. Peter discussed this at Pentecost in Acts 2:23, when he stated, "This Jesus, delivered up according to the definite plan and foreknowledge of God, you crucified and killed by the hands of lawless men." God did not force these men to act against their wills. They did what they wanted to do and were totally responsible for their actions. God, however, is so awesome that He was able to bring about His eternal plan for the salvation of mankind through the willing choices of the Jewish mob.

A Choice in Salvation?

If God is sovereign over everything, does that mean He is also sovereign over the salvation of His people? The Bible holds that "God's choice of certain individuals unto salvation before the foundation of the world rested solely in His own sovereign will. His choice of particular sinners was not based on any foreseen response or obedience on their part, such as faith, repentance, etc. On the contrary, God gives faith and repentance to each individual whom He selected. These acts are the result, not the cause, of God's choice. . . . God's choice of the sinner, not the sinner's choice of Christ is the ultimate cause of salvation."[3]

This doctrine of unconditional election is also known as predestination, a word that sends chills up the spines of those who do not understand it. But those who reject this doctrine must ask themselves what kind of a God they want to believe in: a God who is in control of everything or one who is at the mercy of man and his decisions?

Think on these Scripture passages that support unconditional election:

"I will be gracious to whom I will be gracious, and will show mercy on whom I will show mercy." (Ex. 33:19b)

Blessed is the nation whose God is the LORD, the people whom he has chosen as his heritage! (Ps. 33:12)

Our God is in the heavens; he does all that he pleases. (Ps. 115:3)

"No one knows the Father except the Son and anyone to whom the Son chooses to reveal him." (Matt. 11:27b)

"For many are called, but few are chosen." (Matt. 22:14)

"And if the Lord had not cut short the days, no human being would be saved. But for the sake of the elect, whom he chose, he shortened the days." (Mark 13:20)

"I am not speaking of all of you; I know whom I have chosen." (John 13:18a)

"You did not choose me, but I chose you and appointed you that you should go and bear fruit and that your fruit should abide, so that whatever you ask the Father in my name, he may give it to you." (John 15:16)

And when the Gentiles heard this, they began rejoicing and glorifying the work of the Lord, and as many as were appointed to eternal life believed. (Acts 13:48b)

And we know that for those who love God all things work together for good, for those who are called according to his purpose. For those whom he foreknew he also predestined to be conformed to the image of his Son, in order that he might be the firstborn among many brothers. (Rom. 8:28–29)

Though they were not yet born and had done nothing either good or bad—in order that God's purpose of election might continue, not because of works but because of him who calls—she was told, "The older will serve the younger." As it is written, "Jacob I loved, but Esau I hated." (Rom. 9:11–13)

So then it depends not on human will or exertion, but on God, who has mercy. (Rom. 9:16)

So then he has mercy on whomever he wills, and he hardens whomever he wills. (Rom 9:18)

He chose us in him before the foundation of the world, that we should be holy and blameless before him. (Eph. 1:4)

He predestined us for adoption through Jesus Christ, according to the purpose of his will. (Eph. 1:5)

God chose you as the firstfruits to be saved, through sanctification by the Spirit and belief in the truth. To this he called you through our gospel, so that you may obtain the glory of our Lord Jesus Christ. (2 Thess. 2:13b–14)

Paul, a servant of God and an apostle of Jesus Christ, for the sake of the faith of God's elect and their knowledge of the truth. (Titus 1:1a)

And all who dwell on earth will worship it, everyone whose name has not been written before the foundation of the world in the book of life of the Lamb that was slain. (Rev. 13:8)

We can now rejoice in the comfort of knowing that God is sovereign in all things, including our salvation. This is truly a marvelous, life-changing truth!

Where does this leave us? Are you now beginning to see that God is sovereign over all things, even the most minute details of the universe, but that at the same time we all have the ability to choose what we desire? If this is true, we are left with one profound question: How awesome can this God really be?

God is much greater than we can possibly imagine. A deity so powerful that He can allow His creatures to make free choices, yet determine from the foundation of time what those choices will be, leaves us in total awe. This truth should make us want to fall on our knees in total praise and submission to Him.

At the same time, this truth should bring tears of thankfulness to our eyes. It is nearly incomprehensible that a God this powerful loved you and me enough not only to choose us from the beginning of time, but also to work all things together for our good. Only an all-powerful God could do this.

NOTES

1 Wayne Grudem, *Systematic Theology* (Grand Rapids, Mich.: Zondervan, 1994), 317.

2 Ibid., 321.

3 David N. Steele and Curtis C. Thomas, *The Five Points of Calvinism: Defined, Defended, Documented* (Phillipsburg, N.J.: P&R Publishing, 1963), 16.

Chapter 2

HOW DO I GET TO HEAVEN?

E very human being believes one of two things about an afterlife:

• There is no existence beyond the grave; once we die, we just rot away in the ground and become nothing.

• There is another existence beyond the grave in a "heaven" of some kind.

If you believe the first statement, you have no hope of anything beyond this life. You should be doing everything you possibly can to enjoy your time on this earth. Eat, drink, and be merry, as the Epicurean philosophers of old said, for if there is nothing beyond this life, you are a fool not to try to enjoy this life to its fullest. Put yourself first and live for your own pleasure.

If, on the other hand, you fall into the second category, you are in the great majority of people who have ever lived. Even Eastern religions, such as Buddhism and Hinduism, that believe in reincarnation teach that man will escape the wheel of rebirth and ultimately end up in a nirvana (heaven). The hope and desire for heaven is the greatest motivating factor in human existence. It is what we live for.

So there is broad agreement that there is a "heaven." But the agreement dissolves when we ask, "How do we get there and what does it look like?"

Does each religion have its own path? Is there one way to get there for citizens of the United States and another way for citizens of China, India, Russia, Ethiopia, and Iran? Does each religion have its own "heaven," Nirvana, or nexus? Are there different "heavens" for different people groups? What can I do in this life to get there? Can I earn my way there?

When I sit down next to a person on an airplane, I usually ask, "Which do you want to talk about, politics or religion?" The person invariably picks politics. Once we have exhausted this topic, I say, "OK, now it's time for religion." After finding out what my fellow passenger's basic belief system is, I ask him how he expects to get to heaven. Invariably I receive the same generic, moralistic response: "I live a good life, I am kind to people, I don't lie or steal, I try to follow the Ten Commandments. When I die, God is going to look down on me and say 'good job,' and I will get in."

All the religions of the world, with the exception of Christianity, believe that you can earn your way to heaven through the manner in which you live. This "works righteousness" takes many forms in many different religions, but it all boils down to the same thing. If I try hard to be good or meet some requirements, I can earn favor with the Almighty and he will reward me with heaven when I die.

Sadly, this understanding is wrong. Whether you are a misguided "Christian" trying to earn your salvation through your good works or an adherent of one of the many other world religions attempting to please your deity and earn your way to heaven, you will fail. In the beginning, when God created the first humans, Adam and Eve, he gave them the opportunity to live forever through perfect obedience. That was the requirement—not trying hard, but perfect obedience. They failed, and so would you or I in the same situation.

The correct answer to the question of how to get to heaven is actually very simple: You must have faith and trust in the Lord Jesus Christ, who died for your sins and lived the perfect life for you. There is only one way to heaven, and it is not by good works.

Christianity is an exclusive religion; it teaches that heaven is open only to those who believe in Christ. Sadly, anyone who does not have faith in Christ has no hope of eternal life with God and will spend eternity in hell. This is a fact and should be the primary motivation to spur the believer's desire to evangelize the other religions of the world.

Thousands of books have been written on the means of salvation from all kinds of perspectives, but there is only one perspective that matters: God's.

The One Way to Heaven

Let us look at this question in the words of Jesus Himself, delivered at a time in His life when He had less than a week to live. He wanted to make sure, beyond any doubt, that His disciples knew exactly who He was and how they would get to see Him again someday.

In John 14:1–14, we find Jesus in the upper room of a house in Jerusalem eating His "last supper" with His best friends. He says:

"Let not your hearts be troubled. Believe in God; believe also in me. In my Father's house are many rooms. If it were not so, would I have told you that I go to prepare a place for you? And if I go and prepare a place for you, I will come again and will take you to myself, that where I am you may be also. And you know the way to where I am going." Thomas said to him, "Lord, we do not know where you are going.

How can we know the way?" Jesus said to him, "I am the way, and the truth, and the life. No one comes to the Father except through me. If you had known me, you would have known my Father also. From now on you do know him and have seen him." Philip said to him, "Lord, show us the Father, and it is enough for us." Jesus said to him, "Have I been with you so long, and you still do not know me, Philip? Whoever has seen me has seen the Father. How can you say, 'Show us the Father'? Do you not believe that I am in the Father and the Father is in me? The words that I say to you I do not speak on my own authority, but the Father who dwells in me does his works. Believe me that I am in the Father and the Father is in me, or else believe on account of the works themselves. Truly, truly, I say to you, whoever believes in me will also do the works that I do; and greater works than these will he do, because I am going to the Father. Whatever you ask in my name, this I will do, that the Father may be glorified in the Son. If you ask me anything in my name, I will do it."

These fourteen verses sum up the entire Bible as succinctly as possible:

- We are to believe in Jesus.
- Jesus is God.

- If we believe, we will be with Christ in heaven.
- Belief in Christ is the only way to heaven.
- We should believe because Jesus tells us to or because of the miracles He performed.

This is the gospel message. Christ is God, and to believe in Him is the only way to get to heaven. All other religions are false and deceive those who put their trust in them because they teach false ways to get to heaven. Look at these two additional verses:

Acts 4:12: "And there is salvation in no one else, for there is no other name under heaven given among men by which we must be saved."

First John 5:12: "Whoever has the Son has life; whoever does not have the Son of God does not have life."

What proof do we have that what Jesus said was correct? Why should we believe in Him? How do we know what He said was true? These are great questions for a person who is seeking the truth to ask. There are two main logical reasons to believe in Christ:

1. A multitude of eyewitnesses told the same story. The four Gospel accounts—Matthew, Mark, Luke, and John— are told from different perspectives and to different people groups. Matthew wrote specifically to the Jews, while John wrote more to the Gentiles (non-Jews). All these books, however, tell the same story and never contradict one another. These men lived with Jesus and were eyewitnesses

to His deeds and teachings. In any court of law, four witnesses saying the same thing would prove a case.

2. Jesus performed many miracles that proved His divine nature. From turning water into wine, to healing the blind and the lame, to raising the dead, Jesus did things that no mere man could possible have done. While He cared about the recipients of these miracles, His main purpose in performing them was to prove His deity.

In John 14, Jesus tells His disciples that He is the only way of salvation and how He must go to the Father (die) to bring about this salvation. Then, in verse 29, He says, "Now I have told you before it takes place, so that when it does take place you may believe." He was giving advance notice of what He would do and what it would accomplish so that we would have a way to prove whether or not what He said was true. He spoke these words on Thursday night. On Friday, He was crucified, and on Sunday, He rose from the dead! Everything that Jesus predicted about Himself came true.

Listen to how Jesus explains this in a loving manner to His disciples:

John 16:16–20: "A little while, and you will see me no longer; and again a little while, and you will see me. . . . Truly, truly, I say to you, you will weep and lament, but the world will rejoice. You will be sorrowful, but your sorrow will turn to joy."

John 16:27: "The Father himself loves you, because you

have loved me and have believed that I came from God."

John 17:3: "And this is eternal life, that they know you the only true God, and Jesus Christ whom you have sent."

Matthew 16:16: "Simon Peter replied, 'You are the Christ, the Son of the living God.' And Jesus answered him, 'Blessed are you, Simon Bar-Jonah! For flesh and blood has not revealed this to you, but my Father who is in heaven.'"

These verses demonstrate that Christ is God. He proved His divinity by dying on the cross and rising from the dead three days later, as He promised He would. The only requirement to get to heaven is to believe this truth and trust in Christ to save you from your sins. It is so simple, but it is the truth. Meditate on these verses:

> If you confess with your mouth that Jesus is Lord and believe in your heart that God raised him from the dead, you will be saved. (Rom. 10:9)

> Who is the liar but he who denies that Jesus is the Christ? This is the antichrist, he who denies the Father and the Son. (1 John 2:22–23)

> And this is the promise that he made to us—eternal life. (1 John 2:25)

> By this you know the Spirit of God: every spirit that confesses that Jesus Christ has come in the

flesh is from God, and every spirit that does not confess Jesus is not from God. (1 John 4:2)

Everyone who believes that Jesus is the Christ has been born of God, and everyone who loves the Father loves whoever has been born of him. (1 John 5:1)

For everyone who has been born of God overcomes the world. And this is the victory that has overcome the world—our faith. Who is it that overcomes the world except the one who believes that Jesus is the Son of God? (1 John 5:4–5)

Who Will Be Saved?

Did Christ die on the cross for everyone or only for the people who believe in Him? Is there an elect people of God? Is everybody going to go to heaven or only those who put their faith and trust in Him? Do only those whom Christ chose before the foundation of the earth (the elect) believe in Him? These are thought-provoking questions, and we have God-given answers.

Christ's redeeming work was intended to save the elect only. His work actually secured salvation for them. His death was a substitutionary endurance of the penalty of sin in the place of certain specified sinners. Christ's redemption secured everything necessary for their salvation, including faith, which unites them to Him. The gift of faith is infallibly applied by the Spirit to all for whom Christ died, thereby guaranteeing their salvation.[1]

As Loraine Boettner has written, the atonement (the death of Christ to atone for our sins) "is like a narrow bridge which goes all the way across the stream; rather than a great wide bridge that goes only half-way across."[2] In other words, the Scriptures teach that salvation is complete for some rather than partial for all. This doctrine can be called limited atonement.

Consider these Scripture passages that teach that God actually accomplished redemption for His people:

> "She will bear a son, and you shall call his name Jesus, for he will save his people from their sins." (Matt. 1:21)

> "For this is my blood of the covenant, which is poured out for many for the forgiveness of sins. (Matt. 26:28)

> "I am the good shepherd. I know my own and my own know me, just as the Father knows me and I know the Father; and I lay down my life for the sheep." (John 10:14–15)

> "I am not speaking of all of you; I know whom I have chosen." (John 13:18a)

"You did not choose me, but I chose you and appointed you that you should go and bear fruit and that your fruit should abide, so that whatever you ask the Father in my name, he may give it to you." (John 15:16)

"You have given him authority over all flesh, to give eternal life to all whom you have given him. And this is eternal life, that they know you the only true God, and Jesus Christ whom you have sent." (John 17:2–3)

"I am praying for them. I am not praying for the world but for those whom you have given me, for they are yours. All mine are yours, and yours are mine, and I am glorified in them." (John 17:9–10)

"Father, I desire that they also, whom you have given me, may be with me where I am, to see my glory that you have given me because you loved me before the foundation of the world." (John 17:24)

For if while we were enemies we were reconciled to God by the death of his Son, much more, now that we are reconciled, shall we be saved by his life. (Rom. 5:10)

Grace to you and peace from God our Father and the Lord Jesus Christ, who gave himself for our sins to deliver us from the present evil age, according to the will of our God and Father. (Gal. 1:3–4)

Christ redeemed us from the curse of the law by becoming a curse for us. (Gal. 3:13a)

[Jesus] gave himself for us to redeem us from all lawlessness and to purify for himself a people for his own possession who are zealous for good works. (Titus 2:14)

He himself bore our sins in his body on the tree, that we might die to sin and live to righteousness. By his wounds you have been healed. (1 Peter 2:24)

And they sang a new song, saying, "Worthy are you to take the scroll and to open its seals, for you were slain, and by your blood you ransomed people for God from every tribe and language and people and nation." (Rev. 5:9)

This last verse best sums up the dual truths that we have discussed: belief in Christ is the only way to heaven and Christ Himself has chosen a people to join Him there through faith in Him.

Are We Eternally Secure?

With this said, there is one more question to be answered. God has chosen you for salvation and you have put your faith and confidence in Christ through belief in Him. You are destined for heaven and an eternal life with Christ. Is it possible for you to fall from His grace? This is a big question. It deals with our security on this earth and the comfort that we can have in our future.

The Bible teaches that once a person is truly saved, he is always saved, for he is kept in faith by God: "All who were chosen by God, redeemed by Christ, and given faith by the Spirit are eternally saved. They are kept in faith by the power of Almighty God and thus persevere to the end."[3] This doctrine is called the perseverance of the saints. As Paul writes: "For I am sure that neither death nor life, nor angels nor rulers, nor things present nor things to come, nor powers, nor height nor depth, nor anything else in all creation, will be able to separate us from the love of God in Christ Jesus our Lord" (Rom. 8:38–39).

What about those who attend church for years, give of their time and resources, and show outward signs of faith and repentance, only to end their lives in rebellion and sin? The Bible does not teach that such people have fallen from grace, but that they were never saved in the first place. Jesus said in Matthew 7:21–23: "Not everyone who says to me 'Lord, Lord,' will enter the kingdom of heaven, but the one who does the will of my Father who is in heaven. On that day many will say to me, 'Lord, Lord, did we not prophesy in your name, and cast out demons in your name, and do many mighty works in your name?' And then will I declare to them, 'I never knew you; depart from me, you workers of lawlessness.'"

Meditate on these Scripture passages that undergird the doctrine of the perseverance of the saints:

"For the mountains may depart and the hills be removed, but my steadfast love shall not depart from you, and my covenant of peace shall not be removed," says the LORD, who has compassion on you. (Isa. 54:10)

"What do you think? If a man has a hundred sheep, and one of them has gone astray, does he not leave the ninety-nine on the mountains and go in search of the one that went astray? And if he finds it, truly, I say to you, he rejoices over it more than over the ninety-nine that never went astray. So it is not the will of my Father who is in heaven that one of these little ones should perish." (Matt. 18:12–14)

Whoever believes in the Son has eternal life. (John 3:36a)

"Truly, truly, I say to you, whoever hears my word and believes him who sent me has eternal life. He does not come into judgment, but has passed from death to life." (John 5:24)

"Truly, truly, I say to you, whoever believes has eternal life." (John 6:47)

"My sheep hear my voice, and I know them, and they follow me. I give them eternal life, and they will never perish, and no one will snatch them out of my hand. My Father, who has given them to me, is greater than all, and no one is able to snatch them out of the Father's hand. I and the Father are one." (John 10:27–30)

Those whom he predestined he also called, and those whom he called he also justified, and those whom he justified he also glorified. (Rom. 8:30)

You are not lacking in any spiritual gift, as you wait for the revealing of our Lord Jesus Christ, who will sustain you to the end, guiltless in the day of our Lord Jesus Christ. God is faithful, by whom you were called into the fellowship of his Son, Jesus Christ our Lord. (1 Cor. 1:7–9)

He who raised the Lord Jesus will raise us also with Jesus and bring us with you into his presence. . . . For this light momentary affliction is preparing for us an eternal weight of glory beyond all comparison. (2 Cor. 4:14, 17)

And do not grieve the Holy Spirit of God, by whom you were sealed for the day of redemption. (Eph. 4:30)

For you have died, and your life is hidden with Christ in God. When Christ who is your life appears, then you also will appear with him in glory. (Col. 3:3–4)

The Lord will rescue me from every evil deed and bring me safely into his heavenly kingdom. To him be the glory forever and ever. Amen. (2 Tim. 4:18)

Thus, the Bible is clear that God has chosen a people and that they are safe and secure in His love and protection for eternity. What a fabulous truth God has given us to comfort those who have faith and trust in Him for salvation.

What Is Heaven Like?

I want to conclude this chapter with biblical answers to several questions about heaven. Where is it? Why would I want to go there? Will I enjoy it? How long does it last? The subject of heaven could fill many books, but here I want to help clear up some of the misunderstandings about heaven and eternity. Once you truly comprehend the "facts of heaven" you will be both excited about going there and in awe of God's home.

Heaven is the place where God lives. The Bible calls it the "third heaven." This is actually very logical. The "first heaven" is the sky that we see above us, the "second" is the universe that exists beyond our atmosphere, and the "third" is that area beyond the universe.

Second Corinthians 12:2 says, "I know a man in Christ who fourteen years ago was caught up to the third heaven—whether in the body or out of the body I do not know, God knows."

Recently, I viewed pictures of deep space taken by the Hubble Space Telescope that is orbiting earth. The beauty and grandeur captured in these photos is beyond imagination. The awesomeness of the cosmos, with its expanse of millions of light years, its planets, galaxies, stars, nebulae, and black holes, makes our existence on earth seem small and insignificant. Yet God "lives" beyond all that grandeur.

If you are not in awe of His majesty when pondering these thoughts, you are missing out on a great joy!

The Bible says that when Christians die, our souls go immediately to heaven to be with God and our Savior, Jesus Christ. While this is fabulous news, it can be somewhat of a turnoff if you envision life in heaven as floating around on the clouds in the sky forever like some kind of an angel. This is a wrong interpretation. Heaven is a temporary existence that our souls will enjoy. It will last until Christ comes back to earth, ends this world, and creates "new heavens and a new earth." We will then be reunited with our perfected earthly bodies and live forever with God in this perfect world, living normal lives in His glorious presence.

Matthew 5:5: "Blessed are the meek for they shall inherit the earth."

Second Peter 3:13: "But according to his promise we are waiting for new heavens and a new earth in which righteousness dwells."

Revelation 21:1–4: "Then I saw a new heaven and a new earth, for the first heaven and the first earth had passed away, and the sea was no more. And I saw the holy city, new Jerusalem, coming down out of heaven from God, prepared as a bride adorned for her husband. And I heard a loud voice from the throne saying, 'Behold, the dwelling place of God is with man. He will dwell with them, and they will be his people, and God himself will be with them as their God. He will wipe away every tear from their eyes, and death shall be no more, neither shall there be mourning, nor crying, nor pain anymore, for the former things have passed away.'"

Isaiah 65:17–18: "For behold, I create new heavens and a new earth, and the former things shall not be remembered or come into mind. But be glad and rejoice forever in that which I create; for behold, I create Jerusalem to be a joy, and her people to be a gladness."

The Bible tells us that we will live in the new earth for eternity. How long is eternity? Time will no longer mean anything there. The last verse of the hymn "Amazing Grace" says, "When we've been there ten thousand years, bright shining as the sun, we've no less days to sing God's praise than when we've first begun." In other words, there is no end to life in heaven.

Can you imagine what it will be like to live forever in a perfect environment with God? No sin, no sickness, no fear, no pain, no worries, and no death! This is the life that we have before us if we put our faith and trust in Jesus Christ. No greater gift could possibly be offered.

We are saved by God by His wonderful grace, but we are also saved for a purpose. The next chapter will help us understand how we should live our lives now while believing the future that lies before us.

Notes

1 David N. Steele and Curtis C. Thomas, *The Five Points of Calvinism: Defined, Defended, Documented* (Phillipsburg, N.J.: P&R Publishing, 1963), 17

2 Loraine Boettner, from *The Reformed Doctrine of Predestination*, as quoted in Steele and Thomas, *The Five Points of Calvinism*, 40.

3 Boettner, from *The Reformed Doctrine of Predestination*, as quoted in Steele and Thomas, *The Five Points of Calvinism*, 18.

Chapter 3

HOW SHOULD I LIVE
MY LIFE ON THIS EARTH?

Since God is sovereign over His creation, what is my motivation for life? Since we are saved by grace and not by works, why should we do anything good? What purpose do good works serve? Are there rewards in heaven for what we do here on earth?

True Christians understand that salvation is entirely of God and is not influenced by our good works:

> For by grace you have been saved through faith. And this is not your own doing; it is the gift of God, not a result of works, so that no one may boast. For we are his workmanship, created in Christ Jesus for

good works, which God prepared beforehand, that we should walk in them. (Eph. 2:8–10)

He saved us, not because of works done by us in righteousness, but according to his own mercy, by the washing of regeneration and renewal of the Holy Spirit, whom he poured out on us richly through Jesus Christ our Savior, so that being justified by his grace we might become heirs according to the hope of eternal life. The saying is trustworthy, and I want you to insist on these things, so that those who have believed in God may be careful to devote themselves to good works. These things are excellent and profitable for people. (Titus 3:5–8)

These passages make it clear that our works contribute nothing to our salvation. The work of redemption (a purchase at a price) was accomplished by Christ alone when He sacrificed His life.

However, this understanding can leave Christians inadequately motivated to perform good works. Since we do not need to do good works to earn our salvation, what is our motivation for living as God commands?

Scripture gives us four main reasons to do good works even after we are convinced that we are saved by grace alone.

The Command of God

First, we should do good works because God tells us to. The Bible is filled with statements from God telling His people to behave or live in a certain manner. The Ten Commandments in the Old Testament are prime examples of God's direction in this regard. As Christians, that is all the motivation we should need. If our Creator tells us to do something, we should do it.

We could look at any number of passages that deal with this subject, but we will focus on three biblical books: Matthew, Galatians, and James. Jesus' Sermon on the Mount, recorded in Matthew 5–7, is filled with instructions on how we are to live. One excellent summary is found in 5:14–16: "You are the light of the world. A city set on a hill cannot be hidden. Nor do people light a lamp and put it under a basket, but on a stand, and it gives light to all in the house. In the same way, let your light shine before others, so that they may see your good works and give glory to your Father who is in heaven."

The other two books I have chosen, Galatians and James, have long been thought by some to contradict each other. Here is the dilemma: Paul says in Galatians 3:11, "Now it is evident that no one is justified before God by the law, for 'The righteous shall live by faith.'" Then we have James 2:24, which says, "You see that a person is justified by works and not by faith alone." At first glance, these verses appear contradictory, but they are not. Paul and James are in complete agreement. Both are saying that a true Christian will do good works, and if someone who claims to be a Christian does not do good works, he has never been saved by faith.

Let's look at some other verses from Matthew, Galatians, and James that call us to do good works so as to please our Father in heaven:

> "So if you are offering your gift at the altar and there remember that your brother has something against you, leave your gift there before the altar and go. First be reconciled to your brother, and then come and offer your gift." (Matt. 5:23–24)

> "You have heard that it was said, 'An eye for an eye and a tooth for a tooth.' But I say to you, Do not resist the one who is evil. But if anyone slaps you on the right cheek, turn to him the other also. And if anyone would sue you and take your tunic, let him have your cloak as well. And if anyone forces you to go one mile, go with him two miles. Give to the one who begs from you, and do not refuse the one who would borrow from you." (Matt. 5:38–42)

> "You have heard that it was said, 'You shall love your neighbor and hate your enemy.' But I say to

you, Love your enemies and pray for those who persecute you." (Matt. 5:43–44)

For you were called to freedom, brothers. Only do not use your freedom as an opportunity for the flesh, but through love serve one another. For the whole law is fulfilled in one word: "You shall love your neighbor as yourself." (Gal. 5:13–14)

But I say, walk by the Spirit, and you will not gratify the desires of the flesh. (Gal. 5:16)

Bear one another's burdens, and so fulfill the law of Christ. (Gal. 6:2)

And let us not grow weary of doing good, for in due season we will reap, if we do not give up. So then, as we have opportunity, let us do good to everyone, and especially to those who are of the household of faith. (Gal. 6:9–10)

Know this, my beloved brothers: Let every person be quick to hear, slow to speak, slow to anger; for the anger of man does not produce the righteousness of God. Therefore put away all filthiness and rampant wickedness and receive with meekness the implanted word, which is able to save your souls. But be doers of the word, and not hearers only, deceiving yourselves. For if anyone is a hearer of the word and not a doer, he is like a man who looks intently at his natural face in a mirror. For he looks at himself and goes away and at once forgets what he was like. But the one who looks into the perfect law, the law of liberty, and perseveres, being no hearer who forgets but a doer who acts, he will be blessed in his doing. If anyone thinks he is religious and does not bridle his tongue but deceives his heart, this person's religion is worthless. Religion that is pure and undefiled before God, the Father, is this: to visit orphans and widows in their affliction, and to keep oneself unstained from the world. (James 1:19–27)

If you really fulfill the royal law according to the Scripture, "You shall love your neighbor as yourself," you are doing well. (James 2:8)

So speak and so act as those who are to be judged under the law of liberty. (James 2:12)

These verses make it clear that God expects good works to mark the lives of His redeemed people.

Appreciation for God

Second, we should do good works out of appreciation for what God has done for us. Unfortunately, this motivation does not always compel us as it should. It is easier for us to do something because we think we are going to get a reward for it rather than because we want to express thankfulness for what someone else has done for us.

I know that if I say to one of my children, "Would you please mow the yard out of thankfulness for all the food and lodging that you are receiving?" I will get a less-enthusiastic response than if I say, "Would you mow the yard for $20?" The difference is a reflection of our sinful human natures. We are much more motivated to do good deeds to supposedly earn our way to heaven than to show appreciation for Christ's death on the cross for us.

God wants us to regard Him as our heavenly "Father," a loving being who has chosen us to be His sons and followers. Romans 8:14–17a says: "For all who are led by the Spirit of God are sons of God. For you did not receive the spirit of slavery to fall back into fear, but you have received the Spirit of adoption as sons, by whom we cry, 'Abba! Father!' The Spirit himself bears witness with our spirit that we are children of God, and if children, then heirs—heirs of God and fellow heirs with Christ." As sons of God, we need to live in appreciation for that blessed relationship and try to do good works out of a thankful heart.

Consider also 1 Corinthians 6:19b–20: "You are not your own, for you were bought with a price. So glorify God in your body." Here again we are reminded that God has done something spectacular for us. What more motivation do we need to attempt to please Him and live the Christian life that the Bible describes? The following verses encourage us to appreciation and thankfulness:

"And let the peace of Christ rule in your hearts, to which indeed you were called in one body. And be thankful. Let the work of Christ dwell in you richly, teaching and admonishing one another in all wisdom, singing psalms and hymns and spiritual songs, with thankfulness in your hearts to God." (Col. 3:15–16)

"Let them thank the LORD for his steadfast love, for his wondrous works to the children of men." (Ps. 107:8).

"But we your people, the sheep of your pasture, will give thanks to you forever; from generation to generation we will recount your praise." (Ps. 79:13)

"Oh give thanks to the LORD, for he is good; for his steadfast love endures forever!" (Ps. 118:1)

"But thanks be to God, that you who were once slaves of sin have become obedient from the heart to the standard of teaching to which you were committed, and, having been set free from sin, have become slaves of righteousness." (Rom. 6:17)

"[Give] thanks always and for everything to God the Father in the name of our Lord Jesus Christ." (Eph. 5:20)

"Give thanks in all circumstances; for this is the will of God in Christ Jesus for you." (1 Thess. 5:18)

Fear of the Lord

Third, we should do good works out of an intelligent fear of the Lord. In this case, fear may best be described as reverence. It is the knowledge that we are in the presence of an all-powerful being. Proverbs 1:7 says, "The fear of the LORD is the beginning of knowledge; fools despise wisdom and instruction." We should have a healthy apprehension about how God will react if we do not practice obedience.

While we like to talk about the love of God, the Bible actually has more to say about His wrath. That wrath is mentioned in some of the following verses, which make it very clear that we need to live in a healthy fear of God that encourages us to do good works:

"Gather the people to me, that I may let them hear my words, so that they may learn to fear me all the days that they live on the earth, and that they may teach their children so." (Deut. 4:10b)

"Now this is the commandment, the statutes and the rules that the LORD your God commanded me to teach you, that you may do them in the land to which you are going over, to possess it, that you may fear the LORD your God, you and your son and your son's son, by keeping all his statutes and his commandments, which I command you, all the days of your life, and that your days may be long." (Deut. 6:1–2)

"Now therefore fear the LORD and serve him in sincerity and in faithfulness." (Josh. 24:14a)

"And he said to man, 'Behold, the fear of the Lord, that is wisdom, and to turn away from evil is understanding.'" (Job 28:28)

Serve the LORD with fear, and rejoice with trembling. (Ps. 2:11)

Oh, how abundant is your goodness, which you have stored up for those who fear you. (Ps. 31:19a)

Oh, fear the LORD, you his saints, for those who fear him have no lack! (Ps. 34:9)

For as high as the heavens are above the earth, so great is his steadfast love toward those who fear him. (Ps. 103:11)

Blessed is everyone who fears the LORD, who walks in his ways! (Ps. 128:1)

Fear God and keep his commandments, for this is the whole duty of man. (Eccl. 12:13b)

"And do not fear those who kill the body but cannot kill the soul. Rather fear him who can destroy both soul and body in hell." (Matt. 10:28)

"In every nation anyone who fears him and does what is right is acceptable to him." (Acts 10:35)

For we must all appear before the judgment seat of Christ, so that each one may receive what is due for what he has done in the body, whether good or evil. (2 Cor. 5:10)

Do you see the active verbs in these quotes: *serve, turn away, rejoice, walk, keep*, and *do*? Christianity is not a passive religion. We are to be actively doing good works that please God. And one of the primary reasons for doing them is to avoid the wrath of the almighty and righteous God on our lives.

Hebrews 12:5–6 (a quotation of Prov. 3:11–12) says: "My son, do not regard lightly the discipline of the Lord, nor be weary when reproved by him. For the Lord disciplines the one he loves, and chastises every son whom he receives." God will change us and mold us into the people He wants us to be. However, we should strive to become those people voluntarily rather than wait for God to force us to see the right path through His perfect discipline.

Our goal in the world, our "chief end," as the Westminster Shorter Catechism (written in the 1600s and still the most accurate summary of Scripture) proclaims, is to "glorify God and enjoy him forever." Every good work that we do in this world is a form of worship that glorifies God and helps to mold our lives in conformity to His will. The fear of the Lord helps to motivate us to live godly lives, triumphing over our sinful natures.

Rewards in Heaven

The fourth and final reason we should do good works may surprise you. It surprised me when I first realized it. It is to store up for ourselves rewards in heaven.

In his book *Now, That's a Good Question!* R. C. Sproul considers the question many of you may be asking: "Are there gradations in heaven whereby one Christian, as a result of a lifetime of good works, has a higher rank or better quality of existence . . . than someone who just squeaks through at his last breath?" He answers this question as follows:

> This may come as a surprise to many people, but I would answer that question with an emphatic yes. There are degrees of reward that are given in heaven. I'm surprised that this answer surprises so many people. I think there's a reason Christians are shocked when I say there are various levels of heaven as well as gradations of severity of punishment in hell.
>
> We owe much of this confusion to the Protestant emphasis on the doctrine of justification by faith alone. We hammer away at that doctrine, teaching emphatically that a person does not get to heaven through his good works. Our good works give us no merit whatsoever, and the only way we can possibly enter heaven is by faith in Christ, whose merits are given to us. We emphasize this doctrine to the extent that people conclude good works are insignificant and have no bearing at all upon the Christian's future life.
>
> The way historic Protestantism has spelled it out is that the only way we get into heaven is through the work of Christ, but we are promised rewards in heaven according to our works. Saint Augustine,

in his autobiography, "Confessions," said that it's only by the grace of God that we ever do anything even approximating a good work, and none of our works are good enough to demand that God reward them. The fact that God has decided to grant rewards on the basis of obedience or disobedience is what Augustine called God's crowning his own works within us. If a person has been faithful in many things through many years, then he will be acknowledged by his Master, who will say to him, "Well done, thou good and faithful servant." The one who squeaks in at the last moment has precious little good works for which he can expect reward.

I think the gap between tier one and tier ten in heaven is infinitesimal compared to the gap in getting there or not getting there at all. Everybody's cup in heaven is full, but not everybody in heaven has the same size cup. Again, it may be surprising to people, but I'd say there are at least twenty-five occasions where the New Testament clearly teaches that we will be granted rewards according to our works. Jesus frequently holds out the reward motif as the carrot in front of the horse—"great will be your reward in heaven" if you do this or that. We are called to work, to store up treasures for ourselves in heaven, even as the wicked, as Paul tells us in Romans, "treasure up wrath against the day of wrath."[1]

Likewise, in his book titled *The Bible on the Life Hereafter*, William Hendriksen writes:

"But surely in heaven we shall all be equal," says someone. I answer, yes, in the sense that all who enter there will have been sinners who are then in the state of having been "saved by grace." All, moreover, will owe their salvation equally to the sovereign love of God. And the goal for all will be the same, to glorify God and enjoy Him forever. Nevertheless, there will be inequalities, differences, degrees of reward, and in hell degrees of woe. Scripture teaches this doctrine of degrees of glory. When Jesus comes to reward His servants, one of these faithful ones will in the end have ten talents, another four talents. There will be those in the life hereafter who will receive a reward, which others, though saved, will not receive, that is, not in equal measure. Are there not differences among the angels? Is every angel an archangel?[2]

These statements from Sproul and Hendriksen have strong scriptural support. Consider these passages:

"Therefore whoever relaxes one of the least of these commandments and teaches others to do the same will be called least in the kingdom of heaven, but whoever does them and teaches them will be called great in the kingdom of heaven." (Matt. 5:19)

"Do not lay up for yourselves treasures on earth, where moth and rust destroy and where thieves break in and steal, but lay up for yourselves treasures in heaven, where neither moth nor rust destroys and where thieves do not break in and steal. For where your treasure is, there your heart will be also." (Matt. 6:19–21)

"But I tell you, it will be more bearable on the day of judgment for Tyre and Sidon than for you. And you, Capernaum, will you be exalted to heaven? You will be brought down to Hades. For if the mighty works done in you had been done in Sodom, it would have remained until this day. But I tell you that it will be more tolerable on the day of judgment for the land of Sodom than for you." (Matt. 11:22–24)

"Woe to you, scribes and Pharisees, hypocrites! For you devour widows' houses and for a pretense you make long prayers; therefore you will receive the greater condemnation." (Matt. 23:14)

"And he who had received the five talents came forward, bringing five talents more, saying, 'Master, you delivered to me five talents; here I have made five talents more.' His master said to him, 'Well done, good and faithful servant. You have been faithful over a little; I will set you over much. Enter into the joy of your master.' . . . 'For to everyone who has will more be given, and he will have an abundance. But from the one who has not, even what he has will be taken away. And cast the worthless servant into the outer darkness. In that place there will be weeping and gnashing of teeth.'" (Matt. 25:20–21, 29–30)

"And that servant who knew his master's will but did not get ready or act according to his will, will receive a severe beating. But the one who did not know, and did what deserved a beating, will receive a light beating. Everyone to whom much was given, of him much will be required, and from him to whom they entrusted much, they will demand the more." (Luke 12:47–48)

Jesus answered him, "You would have no authority over me at all unless it had been given you from above. Therefore he who delivered me over to you has the greater sin." (John 19:11)

But because of your hard and impenitent heart, you are storing up wrath for yourself on the day of wrath when God's righteous judgment will be revealed. He will render to each one according to his works: to those who by patience in well-doing seek for glory and honor and immortality, he will give eternal life; but for those who are self-seeking and do not obey the truth, but obey unrighteousness, there will be wrath and fury. (Rom. 2:5–8)

According to the grace of God given to me, like a skilled master builder I laid a foundation, and someone else is building upon it. Let each one take care how he builds upon it. For no one can lay a foundation other than that which is laid, which is Jesus Christ. Now if anyone builds on the foundation with gold, silver, precious stones, wood, hay, straw—each one's work will become manifest, for the Day will disclose it, because it will be revealed by fire, and the fire will test what sort of work each one has done. If the work that anyone has built on the foundation survives, he will receive a reward. If anyone's work is burned up, he will suffer loss, though he himself will be saved, but only as through fire. (1 Cor. 3:10–15)

So the prospect of heavenly rewards is a legitimate motivation for good works in this life. However, we must keep certain facts in mind.

First, if we do things in this world strictly to try to get rewards in heaven, we will get nothing. The rewards will be given to the humble servant who does not seek them. These rewards involve God's crowning His own gifts. The rewards are gracious rewards.

Second, once we are in heaven, we will agree with God's decisions concerning who got what rewards, and we will be fully satisfied with our positions for eternity.

Clearly Scripture tells us we were created to do good works (Eph. 2:10). It shows us that God commands good works. It reveals that we should live obedient lives out of thankfulness and out of reverence for God. And it holds out the prospect of rewards in heaven as a result of good works in this life. Even though our deeds contribute nothing to our salvation, we still have abundant motivation to do good.

NOTES

1 R. C. Sproul, *Now, That's a Good Question!* (Wheaton, Ill.: Tyndale House, 1996), 287.

2 William Hendriksen, *The Bible on the Life Hereafter* (Grand Rapids, Mich.: Baker Books, 1959), 93.

Chapter 4

WHAT IS THE PURPOSE OF PRAYER AND EVANGELISM?

Since God has predetermined everything that comes to pass, why should we spend time in prayer or evangelism? John Calvin, one of the leaders of the Protestant Reformation, saw great value in prayer. In fact, he devoted seventy pages to this subject in his book *Institutes of the Christian Religion*. He wrote, "To know God as the master and bestower of all good things, who invites us to request them of him, and still not go to him and not ask of him—this would be of as little profit as for a man to neglect a treasure, buried and hidden in the earth, after it had been pointed out to him."[1]

I believe Scripture gives us at least five great reasons to pray even though God has predetermined everything.

God Commands Prayer

First, God commands it. Is this not reason enough to do anything in this life? In the following verses, God gives us great motivation for prayer and encourages us to come to Him with our problems and desires:

> [Pray] at all times in the Spirit, with all prayer and supplication. To that end keep alert with all perseverance, making supplication for all the saints, and also for me, that words may be given to me in opening my mouth boldly to proclaim the mystery of the gospel. (Eph. 6:18–19)

> Do not be anxious about anything, but in everything by prayer and supplication with thanksgiving let your requests be made known to God. (Phil. 4:6)

> Is anyone among you suffering? Let him pray. (James 5:13a)

We Worship through Prayer

Second, prayer is a means of worshiping God. Any time we do what God desires, we are honoring Him. By coming to God in prayer, we obey His command, thereby showing that we recognize that He is our Lord. Praying is one way to worship

Him and show our submission to Him. Doing it on our knees is a further way of showing humble reverence to Him:

> Be still before the LORD and wait patiently for him. (Ps. 37:7a)

> Praise is due you, O God, in Zion, and to you shall vows be performed. O you who hear prayer, to you shall all flesh come. (Ps. 65:1–2)

> The LORD is far from the wicked, but he hears the prayer of the righteous. (Prov. 15:29)

> Pray without ceasing, give thanks in all circumstances; for this is the will of God in Christ Jesus for you. (1 Thess. 5:17–18)

Prayer Is a Blessing

Third, prayer is a blessing to us. We come away from prayer refreshed with the knowledge that we have met with the almighty God. Prayer is one of the means of grace (along with reading Scripture and hearing the preached Word of God) that we have to communicate with God. Through prayer, we can develop a close relationship with God to the point of being comfortable in talking to Him at any time about anything:

The LORD is near to all who call on him, to all who call on him in truth. (Ps. 145:18)

Draw near to God, and he will draw near to you. (James 4:8a)

We have confidence before God; and whatever we ask we receive from him, because we keep his commandments and do what pleases him. (1 John 3:21b–22)

God Uses Our Prayers

Fourth, God uses prayer to bring about His predetermined will. Prayer does not change God's mind. God not only ordains ends, He ordains the means that He uses to bring about those ends. One of those means is prayer.

In the story of Elijah and the prophets of Baal (1 Kings 18:20–46), we read a fabulous account of how God showed in a dramatic way that He was the only true God. He summoned the 450 prophets of Baal to Mount Carmel for a challenge. Elijah organized a contest in which each side would set up an altar with a sacrifice on it, then pray to its god or God to light the fire under the sacrifice. Elijah let the prophets of Baal go first.

First Kings 18:26 says: "And they took the bull that was given them, and they prepared it and called upon the name of Baal from morning until noon, saying, 'O Baal, answer us!' But there was no voice, and no one answered. And they limped around the altar that they had made."

Elijah then built an altar, prepared his sacrifice, and had the people pour water on it three times so as to make it soaking wet. Then he prayed: "O LORD, God of Abraham, Isaac, and Israel, let it be known this day that you are God in Israel, and that I am your servant, and that I have done all these things at your word" (v. 36). The response was immediate: "Then the fire of the LORD fell and consumed the burnt offering and the wood and the stones and the dust, and licked up the water that was in the trench" (v. 38).

There had been a drought in the land, but after this dramatic display of God's power, Elijah told King Ahab that it was about to rain. Elijah was sure of God's purpose. However, he still prayed anxiously with his head between his knees. He had no fear that his prophecy would be discredited, but he knew it was his duty to lay his desires before God:

> So Ahab went up to eat and to drink. And Elijah went up to the top of Mount Carmel. And he bowed himself down on the earth and put his face between his knees. (1 Kings 18:42)

> This is the confidence that we have toward him, that if we ask anything according to his will he hears us. (1 John 5:14)

Prayer Teaches Us Dependence

Fifth, prayer teaches us to depend on God and His sovereignty rather than ourselves. Prayer can be a daily reminder that we are not in control, but rather in the arms of a loving heavenly Father:

> Consider my affliction and my trouble, and forgive all my sins. (Ps. 25:18)

> Call upon me in the day of trouble; I will deliver you, and you shall glorify me. (Ps. 50:15)

> Hear my cry, O God, listen to my prayer; from the end of the earth I call to you when my heart is faint. Lead me to the rock that is higher than I. (Ps. 61:1–2)

> Then I turned my face to the Lord God, seeking him by prayer and pleas for mercy with fasting and sackcloth and ashes. (Dan. 9:3)

> "Your Father knows what you need before you ask him." (Matt. 6:8b)

> And when he had entered the house, his disciples asked him privately, "Why could we not cast it out?" And he said to them, "This kind cannot be driven out by anything but prayer." (Mark 9:28–29)

The Spirit helps us in our weakness. For we do not know what to pray for as we ought, but the Spirit himself intercedes for us with groanings too deep for words. (Rom. 8:26)

If we confess our sins, he is faithful and just to forgive us our sins and cleanse us from all unrighteousness. (1 John 1:9)

The Bible gives us many great examples of prayer, but we will look briefly at two. First, there is the Lord's Prayer, which teaches us to pray "your will be done, on earth as it is in heaven" (Matt. 6:10). We are instructed here to pray as if we understand that God reigns in this world. By doing so, we are agreeing with the biblical doctrine that God's will is supreme. But we are still praying. God tells us to pray because He uses our prayers to bring about those things He already has determined. How can that be? Is not God much greater than we ever imagined?

A second great prayer in the Bible is found in Acts 4:24–30. In verses 27–28, the disciples said that God "anointed" Herod and Pontius Pilate "to do whatever your hand and your plan had predestined to take place." Then, in verse 29, they concluded by saying, "And now, Lord, look upon their threats and grant to your servants to continue to speak your word with all boldness." Those who were praying here said they knew things were happening the way God had planned them, but they still prayed that He would work in them. They knew that prayer mattered.

We cannot understand this; it is a mystery, like the issue of God's sovereignty and man's responsibility that we discussed in Chapter 1. But the fact that we cannot understand how God can predetermine everything, yet our prayers still matter and are heard, does not mean both facts are not true.

In an article titled "The Prayers of the Righteous Are Never Futile," R. C. Sproul wrote:

> If God is sovereign, why pray? When I pray to God I am talking to One who has all knowledge. One who cannot possibly learn anything from me that He doesn't already know. He knows everything there is to know, including what's on my mind. He knows what I'm going to say to Him before I say it. He knows what He's going to do before He does it. His knowledge is sovereign, as He is sovereign.
>
> People may ask: "Does prayer change God's mind?" To ask such a question is to answer it. What kind of God could be influenced by my prayers? What could my prayers do to induce Him to change His plans? Could I possibly give God any information about anything that He doesn't

already have? Or could I persuade Him toward a more excellent way by my superior wisdom? Of course not. I am completely unqualified to be God's mentor or His guidance counselor. So the simple answer is that prayer does not change God's mind.

"Does prayer change things?" Now, the answer is an emphatic Yes! The Scriptures tell us that "the effective fervent prayer of a righteous man avails much" (James 5:16). What then does prayer change? In the first place, my prayers change me. My time with God is for my edification, not His. Prayer also changes things. In practical terms, we say that prayer works. Prayer is one of the means God uses to bring about the ends He ordains.[2]

We pray expectantly and confidently, not in spite of the sovereignty of God, but because of it. Note these verses:

"Therefore I tell you, whatever you ask in prayer, believe that you have received it, and it will be yours." (Mark 11:24)

That person must not suppose that he will receive anything from the Lord; he is a double-minded man, unstable in all his ways. (James 1:7–8)

Calvin says about these verses, "It is amazing how much our lack of trust provokes God if we request of him a boon that we do not expect."[3] In other words, we need to have reverent confidence that God will answer our prayers, knowing that His answer will always be for our ultimate benefit and His glory.

Our Role in Evangelism

Now let us turn our attention to evangelism. Just as God does not need our prayers, He does not need us to bring about the salvation of His people. However, He grants us the opportunity to witness to others about our faith. The Bible teaches the importance of evangelism and the great honor that we can have as participants in someone's salvation, but it is also clear that it is God who both initiates salvation and works in a person's heart through the Holy Spirit to bring him or her to Himself. We may give the outward call (witness), but God works in the heart:

In addition to the outward general call to salvation which is made to everyone who hears the gospel, the Holy Spirit extends to the elect a special inward call that inevitably brings them to salvation. The external call (which is made to all without distinction) can be, and often is, rejected; whereas the internal call (which is made only to the elect) cannot be refused; it always results in conversion. . . . The Spirit graciously causes the elect sinner to cooperate, to believe, to repent, to come freely and willingly to Christ. God's grace . . . never fails to result in the salvation of those to whom it is extended.[4]

This doctrine is known as irresistible grace, since God's grace (salvation) to the elect (those chosen by God) is irresistible. Ponder these scriptural proofs:

"I will give you a new heart, and a new spirit I will put within you. And I will remove the heart of stone from your flesh and give you a heart of flesh. And I will put my Spirit within you, and cause you to walk in my statutes and be careful to obey my rules." (Ezek. 36:26–27)

In that same hour he rejoiced in the Holy Spirit and said, "I thank you, Father, Lord of heaven and earth, that you have hidden these things from the wise and understanding and revealed them to little children; yes, Father, for such was your gracious will." (Luke 10:21)

"For as the Father raises the dead and gives them life, so also the Son gives life to whom he will." (John 5:21)

"All that the Father gives me will come to me, and whoever comes to me I will never cast out. . . . No one can come to me unless the Father who sent me draws him. And I will raise him up on the last day. It is written in the Prophets, 'And they will all be taught by God.' Everyone who has heard and learned from the Father comes to me." (John 6:37, 44–45)

One who heard us was a woman named Lydia, from the city of Thyatira, a seller of purple goods, who was a worshiper of God. The Lord opened her heart to pay attention to what was said by Paul. (Acts 16:14)

And those whom he predestined he also called, and those whom he called he also justified, and those whom he justified he also glorified. (Rom. 8:30)

He who had set me apart before I was born, and who called me by his grace, was pleased to reveal his Son to me, in order that I might preach him among the Gentiles. (Gal. 1:15–16a)

[I pray] that the God of our Lord Jesus Christ, the Father of glory, may give you a spirit of wisdom and of revelation in the knowledge of him, having the eyes of your hearts enlightened, that you may know what is the hope to which he has called you. (Eph. 1:17–18a)

For by grace you have been saved through faith. And this is not your own doing; it is the gift of God, not a result of works, so that no one may boast. (Eph. 2:8–9)

There is one body and one Spirit—just as you were called to the one hope that belongs to your call. (Eph. 4:4)

Therefore he is the mediator of a new covenant, so that those who are called may receive the promised eternal inheritance. (Heb. 9:15a)

But you are a chosen race, a royal priesthood, a holy nation, a people for his own possession, that you may proclaim the excellencies of him who called you out of darkness into his marvelous light. (1 Peter 2:9)

And we know that the Son of God has come and has given us understanding, so that we may know him who is true; and we are in him who is true, in his Son Jesus Christ. He is the true God and eternal life. (1 John 5:20).

However, while God is sovereign in salvation, He commands that we participate in evangelism and He uses ordinary people like us to accomplish His plan. This is a great honor, and we need to maximize our effort to spread the knowledge and truth about Christ. God is the primary or first cause of everything that happens in the universe. We, however, are the secondary cause, the means God uses to bring about His will.

Scripture is very clear about a Christian's role in reaching unbelievers. The words of Jesus in Matthew 28:18–20, a passage known as the Great Commission, are especially pointed: "All authority in heaven and on earth has been given to me. Go therefore and make disciples of all nations, baptizing them in the name of the Father and of the Son and of the Holy Spirit, teaching them to observe all that I have commanded you. And behold, I am with you always, to the end of the age."

Other verses contain this clear challenge to evangelize:

"He commanded us to preach to the people and to testify that he is the one appointed by God to be judge of the living and the dead." (Acts 10:42)

"You will be a witness for him to everyone of what you have seen and heard." (Acts 22:15)

Preach the word; be ready in season and out of season; reprove, rebuke, and exhort, with complete patience and teaching. (2 Tim. 4:2)

In your hearts honor Christ the Lord as holy, always being prepared to make a defense to anyone who asks you for a reason for the hope that is in you. (1 Peter 3:15a)

How then will they call on him in whom they have not believed? And how are they to believe in him of whom they have never heard? And how are they to hear without someone preaching? And how are they to preach unless they are sent? As it is written, "How beautiful are the feet of those who preach the good news!" (Rom. 10:14–15)

This last verse sums it up well. It is a great privilege to be used by God as a secondary cause to bring someone to faith in Him. You will recall the story of the prophet Jonah from chapter one. He was basically a reluctant secondary cause, but God changed his heart and used him to bring salvation to the city of Nineveh. Have you ever been in a situation where you were presenting the gospel to someone and the correct words flowed out of your mouth even though you were not sure where they came from? Maybe you were able to remember verses that you normally cannot recall or quote a book or sermon that you had read or heard years earlier. God promises to fill our minds with the truth when we are active in spreading His Word (Luke 12:12). Knowing that God is going to use people such as you and me to bring about the salvation of His people should give us all the incentive and motivation we need to be prepared to give a defense of our faith and hope. Spreading "good news" is a fabulous vocation (1 Peter 3:15a).

God Always Gets His Men and Women

What about the person who wants Jesus but isn't wanted by Him? Here is the simple answer: There is no such person! Consider the testimony of Scripture:

> "You will seek me and find me, when you seek me with all your heart. I will be found by you, declares the LORD." (Jer. 29:13–14a)

> "Ask, and it will be given to you; seek, and you will find; knock, and it will be opened to you. For everyone who asks receives, and the one who

seeks finds, and to the one who knocks it will be opened." (Matt. 7:7–8)

"All that the Father gives me will come to me, and whoever comes to me I will never cast out." (John 6:37)

There has never been a person who wanted to be a Christian to whom God said no. The Bible teaches that when a person wants to be a Christian, God already has worked in his heart, and Scripture assures us that "he who began a good work in you will bring it to completion" (Phil. 1:6). This understanding of Scripture eliminates the "worry" aspect of evangelism. Have you ever heard someone say that he is to blame for another person not becoming a Christian because he never talked to that person about Christ or shared the gospel with him or her? God commands us always to be "prepared to make a defense to anyone who asks you for a reason for the hope that is in you" (1 Peter 3:15b), but we do not have to live in fear that a friend or relative will go to hell if we do not do so. If someone is elect, God will find a willing secondary cause to bring that person to Himself. Neither should we worry if we only introduce the gospel to a friend who then moves away. Again, God's promise to complete the good work He begins provides comfort. If God uses a believer to plant a seed, He can bring another to water it.

God has chosen for Himself a people that He brings to full faith in Him by using the willing second causes of this redeemed people. *Wow*, what an awesome God!

NOTES

1 John Calvin, *Institutes of the Christian Religion* (Philadelphia: Westminster Press, 1960), 850.
2 R. C. Sproul, "The Prayers of the Righteous Are Never Futile," *ByFaith* magazine (January/February 2005), 21.
3 Calvin, *Institutes of the Christian Religion*, 863.
4 David N. Steele and Curtis C. Thomas, *The Five Points of Calvinism: Defined, Defended, Documented* (Phillipsburg, N.J.: P&R Publishing, 1963), 18.

Chapter 5

WHERE DID EVIL COME FROM?

I f God is both sovereign and good, how can evil things happen in the world?

Of all the topics covered in this book, the question of evil is probably the most difficult. One major reason is that the origin of evil is not firmly established in the Scriptures. There is a great mystery here.

That fact leaves us with many tough questions: Does God's providence cover all events that occur in history or only the "good" ones? Does anything occur in this world outside of God's sovereign control? Does Satan have a free rein in this world or are his actions within the sovereignty of God?

As we begin to think through these questions, let's consider five events from modern history:

- The tsunami that killed more than two hundred thousand people around the Indian Ocean in December 2004.
- The devastating terrorist attacks on the United States on Sept. 11, 2001.
- The Holocaust in Germany during World War II.
- The earthquake that hit Port-au-Prince, Haiti, in January 2010.
- The slave trade that brought more than six million Africans to the New World.

Were these events within God's providence or outside of it? Those are the only logical options, as these diagrams demonstrate:

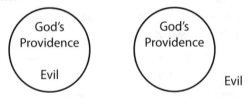

When we listen to the popular media, it is not unusual to hear it said that a good God could not have had anything to do with events such as the tsunami, the attacks of 9/11, the Holocaust, the Haitian earthquake, or the institution of slavery. This is not surprising. These events seem to call God's goodness into question, and some who call themselves believers wish to prevent unbelievers from casting accusations against Him. So they attempt to remove responsibility from God.

But if we say that God's providence does not extend over evil, we are making a strong statement about God. If evil things can happen over which God has no control, what is He like? Thinking this way limits the power of God by casting Him as a being who is at the mercy of His own creation.

When we turn to Scripture, however, we find a very different picture. The Bible tells us that God not only permits evil, He even ordains it:

> Then the LORD said to him, "Who has made man's mouth? Who makes him mute, or deaf, or seeing, or blind? Is it not I, the LORD?" (Ex. 4:11)

> "Shall we receive good from God, and shall we not receive evil?" In all this Job did not sin with his lips. (Job 2:10b)

> "I form light and create darkness, I make well-being and create calamity, I am the LORD, who does all these things." (Isa. 45:7)

> Who has spoken and it came to pass, unless the Lord has commanded it? Is it not from the mouth

of the Most High that good and bad come?
(Lam. 3:37–38)

"Is a trumpet blown in a city, and the people are not afraid? Does disaster come to a city, unless the LORD has done it?" (Amos 3:6)

These verses say that God causes deafness, muteness, and blindness; that He decrees calamities; that trouble comes from Him; and that He causes disasters. This is a difficult, painful reality that is a challenge for us to understand and accept.

Providence Includes Evil

Clearly, nothing is outside the providence of God, and that includes evil. Everything that happens in this world comes from the hand of God. That means Satan does not have a free rein—he can act only within the limits of God's permission. God is not powerless over Satan and evil.

The great news for Christians is found in Romans 8:28: "And we know that for those who love God all things work together for good, for those who are called according to his purpose!"

What is this "good" that the Scriptures mention? Is it our happiness, our financial security, or our success in this life? No, it is none of these. The good that God promises is our ultimate good—the opportunity to live in the new heavens and the new earth with Him for eternity.

Paul knew of this ultimate "good" that is promised to believers, and because of that he could praise God in any circumstance, good or evil, that befell him. He wrote in Philippians 1:21–24: "For to me to live is Christ, and to die is gain. If I am to live in the flesh, that means fruitful labor for me. . . . I am hard pressed between the two. My desire is to depart and be with Christ, for that is far better. But to remain in the flesh is more necessary on your account."

Paul added in 2 Corinthians 4:17–18: "For this slight momentary affliction is preparing for us an eternal weight of glory beyond all comparison, as we look not to the things that are seen but to the things that are unseen. For the things that are seen are transient, but the things that are unseen are eternal."

Let us look briefly at our five examples of evil and see how God could possibly have worked through them to bring about ultimate good (the salvation of His people). This is all supposition because we cannot know the mind of God, but what if:

- a physical disaster claims one life but turns another to God?

- a physical disaster provides the opportunity for a survivor to witness to another and be the means God uses to bring salvation to that person?

• a terrorist attack takes the life of one Christian and sends him or her to heaven while affecting another person in such a way that he turns his life over to Christ?

• through the evil institution of slavery, an entire people were brought to a land where millions of them would become Christians instead of dying as pagans?

God Does No Evil

Although God decrees evil, He does not directly perform morally evil deeds. God cannot do moral evil because His will is directed only toward good. However, God allows Satan, demons, and sinful men to do evil deeds. He does not cause them to do anything they don't want to do; He merely allows them to carry out their evil intentions. Thus, man is responsible for his sin, not God.

As James wrote: "Let no one say when he is tempted, 'I am being tempted by God,' for God cannot be tempted with evil, and he himself tempts no one. But each person is tempted when he is lured and enticed by his own desire. Then desire when it has conceived gives birth to sin, and sin when it is fully grown brings forth death" (James 1:13–15).

What is the most evil and terrible event that has ever occurred? All Christians agree that it was the death of Christ—and the Scriptures make clear that God ordained that event:

"Men of Israel, hear these words: Jesus of Nazareth, a man attested to you by God with mighty works and wonders and signs that God did through him in your midst, as you yourselves know—this Jesus, delivered up according to the definite plan and foreknowledge of God, you crucified and killed by the hands of lawless men." (Acts 2:22–23)

"For truly in this city there were gathered together against your holy servant Jesus, whom you anointed, both Herod and Pontius Pilate, along with the Gentiles and the peoples of Israel, to do whatever your hand and your plan had predestined to take place." (Acts 4:27–28)

God knew that Jesus would be put to death on the cross, for God had designed the atonement. It was His plan that Jesus would die, but evil men actually caused Jesus' death. God ordained the events of Jesus' crucifixion, but man was responsible for the evil that occurred. God did not betray Jesus; Judas did. God did not sentence Jesus to crucifixion; Pilate did. God did not nail Jesus to the cross; the soldiers did.

When Christ died, Satan must have been thinking that he had finally gotten rid of the Son of God. Perhaps he believed he had shown that he was greater than God, for he apparently had spoiled God's plan by killing His Son. But as the Scriptures reveal, God was able to bring "ultimate" good out of that evil event: "For Christ also suffered once for sins, the righteous for the unrighteous, that he might bring us to God, being put to death in the flesh but made alive in the spirit" (1 Peter 3:18).

God's objective is to bring His elect to Himself. If an "evil" event causes that result, whether it is the death of His Son or a natural disaster, we can only rejoice in the end result that He so graciously accomplishes.

One of the best scriptural illustrations of these truths is the story of Joseph and his brothers, found in Genesis 37–50. It is probably the strongest biblical example of the concurrence of the will of God and the will of the creature.

This story is filled with evil events. The first was the sale of Joseph into slavery. This evil was committed by his brothers, but it fulfilled God's purpose to send Joseph to Egypt. The next evil was the false accusation of Joseph by Potiphar's wife, but that fulfilled God's purpose of sending Joseph to prison so he could meet Pharaoh's servants and eventually bring about the salvation of His people. Understanding these things, Joseph could tell his brothers years later, "You meant evil against me, but God meant it for good, to bring it about that many people should be kept alive, as they are today" (Gen. 50:20b).

We cannot see God's purposes. Sometimes He lets us in on a piece or two. But when we see only a part, a particular event may not make sense or we may think that God has made a mistake. God, however, does not make mistakes. Every event that has ever occurred in the history of the world was under His providential control.

The story of Lazarus is another excellent example. Lazarus was the brother of Mary and Martha, two women who were faithful followers of Jesus. Lazarus became very sick, so the sisters sent word to Jesus to come quickly, hoping He would heal their brother.

Oddly, Jesus did not respond right away: "Now Jesus loved Martha and her sister and Lazarus. So, when he heard that Lazarus was ill, he stayed two days longer in the place where he was" (John 11:5–6). Why did Jesus delay if Lazarus was His friend?

Jesus clearly stated the answer in verse 4: "This illness does not lead to death. It is for the glory of God, so that the Son of God may be glorified through it." Jesus allowed His friend to die so that a greater good could be accomplished. He then performed a miracle, raising Lazarus from the dead, to prove He truly was the Son of God.

Questions about the Existence of Evil

There are two big questions with which philosophers have struggled in regard to the existence of evil. The first is this:

"Does the existence of evil prove God does not exist or is not all-powerful?" A secular philosopher could reason as follows:

A wholly good being eliminates all the evil that it can.
If God exists, God is wholly good.
If God exists, He eliminates all the evil that He can.
An omnipotent being can eliminate all evil.
If God exists, God is omnipotent.
If God exists, God can eliminate all evil.
If God exists, God eliminates all evil.
If God exists, there is no evil.
There is evil.
God does not exist.

There are two fundamental problems with the secular philosopher's line of reasoning. First, there is no reason to start with the belief that God, as a wholly good being, would eliminate all the evil that He can. Stating this eliminates the possibility that good can come out of evil events that God controls. The foremost such event was Christ's death on the cross, but Romans 8:28 assures us that all things work for the good of believers—the ultimate good of living with God for eternity. We would not want God to eliminate events that might move us closer to this blessed future.

The second fact that destroys this syllogism is that God does exist. The fact that He has shown Himself, not only in nature but through His personal intervention in this world, not only leaves man without excuse (Rom. 1:20) but destroys this argument by the secular philosopher.

This brings us to the more difficult question, the "why" question: Why does evil exist at all? In other words, if God is good and He created everything, how did evil come into the world?

The Bible tells us that human evil—which is sin, the violation of God's law—began in the Garden of Eden, when Adam and Eve disobeyed God's command not to eat the fruit of the tree of the knowledge of good and evil. But the Bible also provides hints that there was evil in the spiritual realm even earlier. Adam and Eve were tempted to sin by Satan, whom the Bible describes as a fallen angel. Various scriptural passages suggest that Satan and a large number of angels rebelled against God and were condemned by Him (2 Peter 2:4; Jude 6). However, this fact does not explain the origin of the evil to which Satan yielded. He must have been created good (Gen. 1:31), but he somehow conceived the idea of rebelling against God.

There is one thing about which we can be absolutely sure—the source of evil is not God. The Bible declares time after time that God is altogether holy and righteous. He does no evil (Job 34:10) and He hates sin with all His heart

(Deut. 25:16; Ps. 5:4; Luke 16:15). Because He is altogether good, everything He made was good, which rules out the idea that evil was somehow inherent in creation. Likewise, everything He does is good, even though it may appear to be evil or calamitous from the human perspective.

Sproul sums up this truth in his book *Essential Truths of the Christian Faith*:

> If God is able to make everything that happens to us work together for our good, then ultimately everything that happens to us is good. We must be careful to stress here the word *ultimately*. On the earthly plane things that happen to us may indeed be evil. (We must be careful not to call good, evil or evil, good.) We encounter affliction, misery, injustice, and a host of other evils. Yet God in His goodness transcends all of these things and works them to our good. For the Christian, ultimately, there are no tragedies. Ultimately, the providence of God works all these proximate evils for our final benefit.[1]

Evil: The Antithesis of Good

With this understanding and background, how can we best explain the existence of something that God did not create? Everything in this world has an opposite or an antithesis:

white — black
fast — slow
light — dark
smart — stupid
reading this book — not reading this book
me (fill in your name) — not me (fill in someone else's name)

For everything you can possibly think of there is an opposite. In many instances, the opposite is just the nonexistence of the item in question. For example, football—no football, or food—no food.

Opposites are very important. To understand something, you must know its opposite. What would white be if we did not know about black? How could we define smart if we did not understand stupidity? How could we recognize that something is fast if we did not comprehend slowness?

God created everything good. He did not create anything evil. But when He created good, evil automatically came into being as the antithesis or opposite of good. We could not really understand or comprehend "good" if we did not know "evil."

Listen to Paul's amazing thoughts on this subject:

What then shall we say? That the law is sin? By no means! Yet if it had not been for the law, I would not have known sin. I would not have known what it is to covet if the law had not said, "You shall not covet." But sin, seizing an opportunity through the commandment, produced in me all kinds of covetousness. Apart from the law, sin lies dead. I was once alive apart from the law, but when the commandment came, sin came alive and I died. The very commandment that promised life proved to be death to me. For sin, seizing an opportunity through the commandment, deceived me and through it killed me. So the law is holy, and the commandment is holy and righteous and good. Did that which is good, then, bring death to me? By no means! It was sin, producing death in me through what is good, in order that sin might be shown to be sin. (Rom. 7:7–13a)

Paul says here that God's good gift of the law to the human race had the effect of producing sin and death. But these negative effects also revealed the sin that was present in the human heart in order that a solution might be sought through God's redeeming grace. The good revealed the evil, and vice versa.

Sproul touched on this philosophy in his January 2007 Message of the Month lecture:

Evil is always explained or described in negative terms. Evil is a parasite insofar as the parasite depends upon its host for its own existence. Once the host dies, the parasite perishes as well, because the parasite cannot live independently from the host. In that sense, evil is parasitical. It depends on the good for its very definition.

We talk about evil in terms of unrighteousness, imperfection, lawlessness, and disobedience, so that we understand evil only against the background of the prior standard of goodness. Evil is only known insofar as it fails to conform to the standard of goodness.

The very presence of evil bears witness to the prior existence of the good![2]

The great church father Augustine expressed this same theory in his book *Soliloquies*. According to historical theologian Thomas J. Nettles, Augustine argued:

Since God created everything, evil does not have an existence independent of good things. Evil is a privation of good. When all good is gone, nothing exists. Evil is only an absence of good. It is not an independent substance that invades and contaminates, but must borrow from God's good and diminish its glory. The substances in which evil resides are themselves good. Evil is removed not by eradication of a contrary nature . . . but by purifying of the thing itself which was thus depraved. Truth and falsehood dwell in the same tension, according to Augustine, for nothing is false except by some imitation of the true.[3]

Understanding evil as the privation of good or the antithesis of good clears God of creating evil, but allows it to exist in the world and be used by God for His divine purposes.

NOTES

1 R. C. Sproul, *Essential Truths of the Christian Faith* (Carol Stream, Ill.: Tyndale House Publishers, 1992), 50.

2 R. C. Sproul, "The Problem of Evil," Message of the Month CD (Lake Mary, Fla.: Ligonier Ministries, January 2007).

3 Thomas J. Nettles, "Augustine, Doctor of Grace," *Tabletalk* magazine (August 2005), 10.

Chapter 6

WHY DO BAD THINGS HAPPEN TO GOOD PEOPLE?

The first question that we must ask ourselves in this chapter is this: Are there any good people for bad things to happen to?

In what condition are we born into this world? There are basically three possible answers. We were born either good, neutral, or bad. The Bible says that when Adam was put on this earth, he was good, but when he sinned against God, both he and all of his descendants became bad.

> Because of the fall, man is unable of himself to savingly believe the gospel. The sinner is dead, blind, and deaf to the things of God; his heart is deceitful and desperately corrupt. His will is not

free, it is in bondage to his evil nature, therefore, he will not—indeed he cannot—choose good over evil. Consequently, it takes much more than the Spirit's assistance to bring a sinner to Christ—it takes regeneration by which the Holy Spirit makes the sinner [spiritually] alive and gives him a new nature. Faith is not something man contributes to salvation, but is itself a part of God's gift of salvation.[1]

Some Christians believe that man is born sick in sin, but still has enough good in him to choose God. The Bible, however, teaches that man is born corrupt (dead in his sin), so he must be made alive spiritually before he can do anything of a spiritual nature.

The basic issue is whether fallen man has the moral ability to incline himself to the things of God without being regenerated (changed) first. Consider these Scripture passages that teach the fallen state of man and the need for Christ to work in his heart first:

And the LORD God commanded the man, saying, "You may surely eat of every tree of the garden, but of the tree of the knowledge of good and evil you shall not eat, for in the day that you eat of it you shall surely die." (Gen. 2:16–17)

The LORD saw that the wickedness of man was great in the earth, and that every intention of the thoughts of his heart was only evil continually. (Gen. 6:5)

"Who can bring a clean thing out of an unclean? There is not one." (Job 14:4)

Behold, I was brought forth in iniquity, and in sin did my mother conceive me. (Ps. 51:5)

Jesus answered, "Truly, truly, I say to you, unless one is born of water and the Spirit, he cannot enter the kingdom of God. That which is born of the flesh is flesh, and that which is born of the Spirit is spirit. Do not marvel that I said to you, 'You must be born again.'" (John 3:5–7)

"No one can come to me unless the Father who sent me draws him. And I will raise him up on the last day." (John 6:44)

"None is righteous, no, not one; no one understands; no one seeks for God. All have turned aside; together they have become worthless; no one does good, not even one." (Rom. 3:10b–12)

For the mind that is set on the flesh is hostile to God, for it does not submit to God's law; indeed, it cannot. Those who are in the flesh cannot please God. (Rom. 8:7–8)

The natural person does not accept the things of the Spirit of God, for they are folly to him, and he is not able to understand them because they are spiritually discerned. (1 Cor. 2:14)

And you were dead in the trespasses and sins in which you once walked, following the course of this world, following the prince of the power of the air, the spirit that is now at work in the sons of disobedience—among whom we all once lived in the passions of our flesh, carrying out the desires of the body and the mind, and were by nature children of wrath, like the rest of mankind. (Eph. 2:1–3)

And you, who were dead in your trespasses and the uncircumcision of your flesh, God made alive together with him, having forgiven us all our trespasses. (Col. 2:13)

There is no one who is "good" in this world. We are all born "bad," so we all deserve God's wrath and punishment.

The theological term for this state into which we are born is "total depravity." When the Bible teaches that we are all born totally depraved, it does not mean that we are as bad as we can be, but rather that sin has affected every area of our lives. The "total" refers to extent rather than degree.

So, the question of this chapter can now be more accurately phrased: "Why do bad things happen to people who want to do good or want to please God?" In order to help us understand this dilemma, God dedicated an entire book of the Bible to this concern. It is called Job.

Job was a man who had it all (by ancient Near Eastern standards). He had a large family (seven sons and three daughters), seven thousand sheep, three thousand camels, and hundreds of oxen and donkeys (Job 1:2–3). He was wealthy, yet he had a strong faith in God and his future redeemer, Christ. He affirmed, "I know that my Redeemer lives" (19:25).

The Bible tells us that Job was "blameless and upright, one who feared God and turned away from evil" (1:1).

In a discussion between God and Satan, Satan claimed that Job loved and obeyed God only because God had given him prosperity. God told Satan that was not so and allowed Satan a free hand to do whatever he wanted to do to Job as long as he did not take Job's life. Satan used normal physical means (storms, fires, enemies) to kill all of Job's livestock (sheep, donkeys, camels), his ten children, and his servants, and to destroy his home. Job's response was, "The LORD gave, and the LORD has taken away; blessed be the name of the LORD" (1:21).

Next, Satan attacked Job's health and inflicted him with "loathsome sores from the sole of his foot to the crown of his head. And he took a piece of broken pottery with which to scrape himself while he sat in the ashes" (2:7–8). Job's response to this attack on his person was to say: "'Shall we receive good from God, and shall we not receive evil?' In all this Job did not sin with his lips" (2:10).

The remainder of the book of Job is the story of his friends and wife attempting to convince him to "curse God and die" (2:9); in other words, to blame God for his troubles.

Job admitted he did not understand why all this was happening to him. He questioned God and pleaded with Him for answers (he was not aware of the discussions between God and Satan, or the reasons why God was allowing Satan to carry out his plans).

In the end, God appeared in a whirlwind and answered Job, not with an explanation for his suffering but with a description of His own deity. He helped Job see His all-powerful nature, asking, "Where were you when I laid the foundation of the earth" (38:4). God used this description of His power to calm Job's concerns and give him the comfort to put his ultimate faith in the hands of a sovereign and good God. Job responded with trust in God's judgment:

"I know that you can do all things, and that no purpose of yours can be thwarted. 'Who is this that hides counsel without knowledge?' Therefore I have uttered what I did not understand, things too wonderful for me, which I did not know" (42:2–3).

At the conclusion of the story, the Lord restored the fortunes of Job; he was given twice as much as he had before. But that was not the point. The important lesson that the book of Job teaches is that God is in control and that we cannot see the big picture. Bad things that happen to God's people are part of God's ultimate plan to save a people for Himself. We cannot understand each situation, but we can trust God's ultimate result. He promises us in Romans 8:28, "And we know that for those who love God all things work together for good, for those who are called according to his purpose." This good that God is referring to is not earthly prosperity; rather, it is our ultimate good—spending eternity with Him in the new heaven and new earth.

Jesus was confronted with an updated version of the story of Job. Many Jews, like Job's friends, believed that every misfortune in this life was God's punishment for a specific sin. When Jesus encountered a man who had been born blind, He was asked, "Who sinned, this man or his parents, that he was born blind" (John 9:2). Jesus answered, "It is not that this man sinned, or his parents, but that the works of God might be displayed in him" (v. 3).

Jesus used this incident to show that events in the world (pain and suffering) can happen in order to promote the knowledge and glory of God.

This is not meant to dismiss the fact that God does punish sin and that at times we bring problems on ourselves. The life of David after his adultery and murder is a prime example (2 Sam. 12–21). David lost his child with Bathsheba (a woman whom he wrongfully took as his wife after arranging for her husband to be killed in battle) and lived the rest of his life fighting his enemies, who included some of his sons. He had to bear the punishment for his sin but retained the benefits of God's righteousness.

But punishment for sin is not usually the reason why bad things happen to God's people. We do not know the mind and plans of God. We live our lives from man's perspective in faith and trust.

Paul, the greatest theologian in the Bible, sums up life's trials and tribulations in these five profound verses in the book of Romans, Philippians, and Colossians:

> More than that, we rejoice in our sufferings, knowing that suffering produces endurance, and endurance produces character, and character produces hope. (Rom. 5:3–4)

For I consider that the sufferings of this present time are not worth comparing with the glory that is to be revealed in us. (Rom. 8:18)

For it has been granted to you that for the sake of Christ you should not only believe in him but suffer for his sake. (Phil. 1:29)

Indeed, I count everything as loss because of the surpassing worth of knowing Christ Jesus my Lord. For his sake I have suffered the loss of all things and count them as rubbish, in order that I may gain Christ and be found in him, not having a righteousness of my own that comes from the law, but that which comes through faith in Christ, the righteousness from God that depends on faith—that I may know him and the power of his resurrection, and may share his sufferings, becoming like him in his death. (Phil. 3:8–10)

Now I rejoice in my sufferings for your sake, and in my flesh I am filling up what is lacking in Christ's afflictions for the sake of his body, that is, the church. (Col. 1:24)

When we struggle to understand why things happen to us, we need to try to look at the big picture and see things from God's perspective. Let's say I have a major health problem and end up in the hospital. During my stay there, I have the opportunity to witness to a nurse or a doctor who God has placed in my path. That person comes to saving faith and ends up with me in heaven someday. The sickness that I had to endure is therefore more understandable and the pain I suffered more bearable. Who among us would not give up everything that we have in this life if it was the only way of assuring the salvation of even our worst enemy? We will experience great joy someday in heaven when we meet the people for whom our suffering contributed to their eternal life.

Often, our pain and suffering will make no sense until we get to heaven. So we must put our faith and trust in God's divine will and providence, remembering that He loves us and will never give us more than we can bear. Peter helps us to understand this truth in these verses:

> For what credit is it if, when you sin and are beaten for it, you endure? But if when you do good and suffer for it you endure, this is a gracious thing in the sight of God. For to this you have been called, because Christ also suffered for you, leaving you an example, so that you might follow in his steps. (1 Peter 2:20–21)

But even if you should suffer for righteousness' sake, you will be blessed. Have no fear of them, nor be troubled. (1 Peter 3:14)

For it is better to suffer for doing good, if that should be God's will, than for doing evil. (1 Peter 3:17)

But rejoice insofar as you share Christ's sufferings, that you may also rejoice and be glad when his glory is revealed. (1 Peter 4:13)

Therefore let those who suffer according to God's will entrust their souls to a faithful Creator while doing good. (1 Peter 4:19)

And after you have suffered a little while, the God of all grace, who has called you to his eternal glory in Christ, will himself restore, confirm, strengthen, and establish you. (1 Peter 5:10)

No one likes to suffer. If we had our choice, we would all prefer to live lives free of problems, both physical and mental. That, however, is not possible in a sinful world. God never promises us a life of health, wealth, and prosperity. On the contrary, He tells us time and time again that as Christians we will suffer. So the real question is not whether we will suffer but how we will respond to our suffering. Paul tells us to "rejoice in our suffering" (Rom. 5:3). How counter-cultural is that? We can rejoice because we know that the author of our suffering loves us and has a plan for us that will use our suffering for both our and His people's ultimate good.

In the late 1800s, a man by the name of Horatio Spafford was a lawyer in Chicago, a Presbyterian Church elder, and a dedicated Christian. On October 8, 1871, the Great Chicago Fire swept through the city. Spafford, who had invested heavily in real estate, lost almost everything he owned. Two years later, in 1873, Spafford decided his family should take a much-needed vacation in England. After the ship tickets were purchased, Spafford was delayed on business and sent his family ahead of him: his wife, Anna, and his four daughters, Annie, Maggie, Bessie, and Tanetta. They sailed in the steamer Ville du Havre.

On November 22, 1873, the Ville du Havre was struck by a British sailing ship, the Loch Earn. The steamer sank in the midst of the Atlantic Ocean. Anna was saved along with eighty-one of the 307 passengers on board, but all four of Spafford's daughters perished. Upon arriving in Wales, Anna sent a telegram to Spafford saying only: "Saved alone. What shall I do?"

Spafford immediately caught the first ship he could and sailed to England to be with his wife. On his way across the Atlantic, he penned the words to his famous hymn "It is well with My Soul." These are his inspiring words:

When peace, like a river, attendeth my way,
When sorrows like sea billows roll;
Whatever my lot, Thou has taught me to say,
It is well, it is well with my soul.

(Refrain:) It is well (it is well),
With my soul (with my soul),
It is well, it is well with my soul.

Though Satan should buffet, though trials should come,
Let this blest assurance control,
That Christ hath regarded my helpless estate,
And hath shed His own blood for my soul.
(Refrain)

My sin, oh the bliss of this glorious thought!
My sin, not in part but the whole,
Is nailed to His cross, and I bear it no more,
Praise the Lord, praise the Lord, O my soul!
(Refrain)

For me, be it Christ, be it Christ hence to live:
If Jordan above me shall roll,
No pain shall be mine, for in death as in life
Thou wilt whisper Thy peace to my soul.
(Refrain)

And Lord hast the day, when my faith shall be sight,
The clouds be rolled back as a scroll;
The trump shall resound, and the Lord shall descend,
Even so, it is well with my soul.
(Refrain)

Horatio and Anna were blessed with two daughters later in life and spent their remaining days in service to God's kingdom, running soup kitchens, hospitals, and orphanages as part of an American colony in Jerusalem during World War I. They understood what Job, Jesus, Paul, and Peter understood: that God's plans are not known to man, but trust and faith in His results is our calling as Christians. We live not for this life but for the next: "Now faith is the assurance of things hoped for, the conviction of things not seen" (Heb. 11:1).

NOTE

1 David N. Steele and Curtis C. Thomas, *The Five Points of Calvinism: Defined, Defended, Documented* (Phillipsburg, N.J.: P&R Publishing, 1963), 16.

Chapter 7

WHAT HAPPENS
TO BABIES WHO DIE?

I f people are born totally depraved, where do babies go when they die?

Sometime in your life you will know someone, Christian or non-Christian, who had a miscarriage, suffered the death of an infant, or chose to have an abortion. What will you tell that person when he or she asks you where that baby is spending eternity? What will be the basis for your answer?

Assuming that people who die go to either heaven or hell, there are five possibilities for what happens to babies who die:

1. They all go to hell. If a person must make a decision to believe in Christ in order to get to heaven, all babies

who die must be condemned, since babies cannot decide to believe in Christ.

2. Those who are baptized go to heaven; all others go to hell. If baptism is necessary for salvation and actually guarantees salvation, babies who are given the sacrament of baptism and then die go to heaven. Those who do not receive baptism and then die go to hell.

3. Covenant babies (children of believers) go to heaven; all others go to hell. This belief is based on the promise God gave when He made a covenant with Abraham: "I will establish my covenant between me and you and your offspring after you" (Gen. 17:7a). Since children are included in the covenant, this hints that their eternal destinies are secure.

4. Those who are elect (chosen by God) go to heaven; all others go to hell. We have no more idea who the elect babies are than who the elect adults are.

5. They all go to heaven. Because of special grace of God, all babies who die, whether born of Christian or non-Christian parents, get to heaven. This is another way of saying that all babies who die are elect.

There are Christians who hold to each of these views. This disagreement is understandable because the Bible is not explicit in its answer to the question of what becomes of babies who die.

Salvation by Grace Alone

We must admit that babies are not free from the curse of original sin. All children are conceived as sinners and are born morally corrupt (totally depraved), not good or neutral. They may be innocent of personal sin, but they are not innocent of the imputed sin of Adam, just as Scripture teaches:

> "I will never again curse the ground because of man, for the intention of man's heart is evil from his youth." (Gen. 8:21b)

> Behold, I was brought forth in iniquity, and in sin did my mother conceive me. (Ps. 51:5)

> The wicked are estranged from the womb; they go astray from birth, speaking lies. (Ps. 58:3)

> Enter not into judgment with your servant, for no one living is righteous before you. (Ps. 143:2)

> Surely there is not a righteous man on earth who does good and never sins. (Eccl. 7:20)

> "None is righteous, no, not one." (Rom. 3:10)

We all once lived in the passions of our flesh, carrying out the desires of the body and the mind, and
were by nature children of wrath, like the rest of
mankind. (Eph. 2:3)

Since all babies are born depraved, it is logical to
assume that all babies who die go to hell. After all, they
cannot repent or believe in Jesus. As Christians, shouldn't
we believe that no babies who die are elect, since God
obviously did not choose them to live and become Christians? Biblical theology holds that the answer to this
question is "No."

Christians believe that we are saved exclusively by
grace. Fallen, sinful, guilty, depraved children who die have
no merit of their own. Like adults, they must be saved by
grace. Christ bore the sins of all those who would believe
and of all who could not. The fact that infants are too
young to respond to that grace with faith is immaterial.
Grace is based on no merit of any kind within the sinner.
Salvation is based on God's sovereign choice, for adults as
well as infants. All are saved by grace.

But how is God's grace applied to infants who die?
Contemporary Presbyterian theologian R. C. Sproul writes:

We hope and have a certain level of confidence that
God will be particularly gracious toward those who

have never had the opportunity to be exposed to the gospel, such as infants and children who are too disabled to hear and understand. The New Testament does not teach us this explicitly. It does tell us a lot about the character of God—about His mercy and grace—and gives us every reason to have that kind of confidence in His dealings with children.[1]

Charles H. Spurgeon, the great Reformed Baptist preacher of nineteenth-century London, held that all those who perish in infancy are necessarily among the elect, and are therefore received by God:

Among the gross falsehoods which have been uttered against the Calvinists proper is the wicked calumny that we hold the damnation of little infants. But a baser lie was never uttered. There may have existed somewhere in some corner of the earth a miscreant (criminal) who would dare to say that there were infants in hell but I have never met with him nor have I met with a man who ever saw such a person. We say with regard to infants, Scripture saith but little, and therefore where Scripture is confessedly scant it is for no man to determine dogmatically, but I think I speak for the entire body or certainly with exceedingly few exceptions, and those unknown to me, when I say we hold that all infants who die are elect of God and are therefore saved, and we look to this as being the means by which Christ shall see of the travail of his soul to a great degree, and we do sometimes hope that thus the multitude of the saved shall be made to exceed the multitude of the lost. Whatever view our friends may hold upon the point, they are not necessarily connected with Calvinistic doctrine. I believe that the Lord Jesus who said that such is the kingdom of heaven doth daily and constantly receive into his loving arms those tender ones who were only shown and then snatched away to heaven.[2]

Likewise, B. B. Warfield, the great Princeton theologian, explained God's relationship to infants in this manner:

The destiny of infants who die is determined irrespective of their choice by an unconditional decree of God suspended for its execution on no act of their own. Their salvation is wrought by an unconditional application of the grace of Christ to their souls through the immediate and irresistible cooperation of the Holy Spirit prior to and apart from any action of their own proper wills. If death in infancy does depend on God's providence, it is assuredly God in His providence who selects this vast multitude to be made participants of His own conditional salvation. This is but to say that they are unconditionally predestined to salvation from the foundation of the world.[3]

I see ample reason to hope, based on the Bible's teaching about God's character traits of grace and mercy, that He does indeed receive all dying infants into His presence. Since the Bible is not explicit on this question, I have varying degrees of confidence in my conviction as follows: I am "convinced" that all elect babies who die go to heaven. I "believe" that all babies of Christian parents are elect. And I "hope" and "trust" that God saves all babies who die by His perfect grace. In the remainder of this chapter, I will share some reasons why I hold these positions.

Scriptural Reasons for Hope

As both Sproul and Spurgeon note in their comments above, there is no explicit teaching on the eternal destination of dying babies. But Scripture nevertheless gives us much reason to hope that they are saved. One strong scriptural support for the salvation of dying infants is God's attitude toward children. Clearly He has a special care for them:

You are he who took me from the womb; you made me trust you at my mother's breasts. On you was I cast from my birth, and from my mother's womb you have been my God. (Ps. 22:9–10)

"Before I formed you in the womb I knew you, and before you were born I consecrated you." (Jer. 1:5a)

He . . . had set me apart before I was born, and . . . called me by his grace. (Gal. 1:15)

These verses show that God has a great love for little ones. He knows them, He cares about them, and He is committed to saving them.

The best example of this divine love for children may be Psalm 139:1–17:

O LORD, you have searched me and known me! You know when I sit down and when I rise up; you discern my thoughts from afar. You search out my path and my lying down and are acquainted with all my ways. Even before a word is on my tongue, behold, O LORD, you know it altogether. You hem me in, behind and before, and lay your hand upon me. Such knowledge is too wonderful for me; it is high; I cannot attain it. Where shall I go from your

Spirit? Or where shall I flee from your presence? If I ascend to heaven, you are there! If I make my bed in Sheol, you are there! If I take the wings of the morning and dwell in the uttermost parts of the sea, even there your hand shall lead me, and your right hand shall hold me. If I say "Surely the darkness shall cover me, and the light about me be night," even the darkness is not dark to you; the night is bright as day, for darkness is as light with you. For you formed my inward parts; you knitted me together in my mother's womb. I praise you, for I am fearfully and wonderfully made. Wonderful are your works; my soul knows it very well. My frame was not hidden from you, when I was being made in secret, intricately woven in the depths of the earth. Your eyes saw my unformed substance; in your book were written, every one of them, the days that were formed for me, when as yet there were none of them. How precious to me are your thoughts, O God! How vast is the sum of them!

In that final sentence, David affirmed that his earlier statements were a treasured truth. The fact that God knew him before the world was created and while he was in his mother's womb was wonderful to consider.

During the time of His incarnation, Jesus exhibited this

same care for little ones: "Jesus said, 'Let the little children come to me and do not hinder them, for to such belongs the kingdom of heaven.' And he laid his hands on them" (Matt. 19:14–15). Placing His hands on the children was Jesus' way of giving them His blessing. Clearly He felt a special care for them.

The best indication that God saves infants of believers who die is found in 2 Samuel 12:15b–23, which records the sad outcome of the story of David's sin with Bathsheba:

> And the LORD afflicted the child that Uriah's wife bore to David, and he became sick. David therefore sought God on behalf of the child. And David fasted and went in and lay all night on the ground. And the elders of his house stood beside him, to raise him from the ground, but he would not, nor did he eat food with them. On the seventh day the child died. And the servants of David were afraid to tell him that the child was dead, for they said, "Behold, while the child was yet alive, we spoke to him, and he did not listen to us. How then can we say to him the child is dead? He may do himself some harm." But when David saw that his servants were whispering together, David understood that the child was dead. And David said to his servants, "Is the child dead?" They said, "He is dead."

Then David arose from the earth and washed and anointed himself and changed his clothes. And he went into the house of the LORD and worshiped. He then went to his own house. And when he asked, they set food before him, and he ate. Then his servants said to him, "What is this thing that you have done? You fasted and wept for the child while he was alive; but when the child died, you arose and ate food." He said, "While the child was still alive, I fasted and wept, for I said, 'Who knows whether the LORD will be gracious to me, that the child may live.' But now he is dead. Why should I fast? Can I bring him back again? I shall go to him, but he will not return to me."

Hope replaced sorrow in David's heart. He knew where he was going when he left this earth. In Psalm 23:6, David declared, "Surely goodness and mercy shall follow me all the days of my life, and I shall dwell in the house of the LORD forever." And just as David knew he would be taken to heaven someday, he knew he would see his son there. He had total confidence that this infant who had died was with God.

David had other sons, one of whom was Absalom, who led a rebellion against his father and God. When Absalom finally fell in battle and David received the news, he reacted in this way: "And the king was deeply moved and went up to the chamber over the gate and wept. And as he went, he said, 'O my son Absalom, my son, my son Absalom! Would I had died instead of you, O Absalom, my son, my son!'" (2 Sam. 18:33).

The king was deeply moved and he wept. This was the opposite of his reaction when the baby died. David knew that Absalom was not in heaven, so he had great sorrow. He would have preferred to have died himself so that Absalom could keep living, since life on this earth was all that Absalom had.

Another Old Testament story implies God saves infants of nonbelievers. It concerns Jeroboam, a wicked king of Israel who worshiped other gods. He also had a son, Abijah, who became very ill. At that time, God said:

"Thus says the Lord, the God of Israel: . . . 'Behold, I will bring harm upon the house of Jeroboam and will cut off from Jeroboam every male, both bond and free in Israel, and will burn up the house of Jeroboam, as a man burns up dung until it is all gone. Anyone belonging to Jeroboam who dies in the city the dogs shall eat, and anyone who dies in the open country the birds of the heavens shall eat, for the LORD has spoken it.' Arise therefore, go to your house. When your feet enter the city, the child shall die. And all Israel shall mourn for him and bury him, for he only of Jeroboam shall come to the grave, because in him there is found something pleasing to the LORD, the God of Israel, in the house of Jeroboam." (1 Kings 14:7–13)

The baby was saved, but the rest of the household was damned. God found something "pleasing" in an infant of nonbelieving parents.

Additional Scriptural Implications

Here are four additional scriptural teachings that strongly imply that all babies who die go to heaven:

First, have you ever heard someone say, "I wish I had never been born"? Well, characters in the Bible express that thought from time to time:

"Why did I not die at birth, come out from the womb and expire?" (Job 3:11)

"Or why was I not as a hidden stillborn child, as infants who never see the light?" (Job 3:16)

If a man fathers a hundred children and lives many years, so that the days of his years are many, but his soul is not satisfied with life's good things, and he also has no burial, I say that a stillborn child is better off than he. (Eccl. 6:3)

Have you ever wondered about these verses? Why did these men say it is better to die in infancy? Could it be because all babies go to heaven, and these men knew that if they had died as infants, they would have gone directly there? I believe they did. They were rightly expressing a desire to have been with God rather than to have lived trouble-filled lives on this earth.

Second, Scripture records two mass murders of infants. In Exodus 1:22, we read, "Then Pharaoh commanded all his people, 'Every son that is born to the Hebrews you shall cast into the Nile, but you shall let every daughter live.'" And Matthew 2:16–18 says: "Then Herod, when he saw that he had been tricked by the wise men, became furious, and he sent and killed all the male children in Bethlehem and in all that region who were two years old or under, according to the time that he had ascertained from the wise men. Then was fulfilled what was spoken by the prophet Jeremiah: 'A voice was heard in Ramah, weeping and loud lamentation, Rachel weeping for her children; she refused to be comforted, because they are no more.'"

How could a loving God allow these children to be murdered in this manner? Moses was saved by Pharaoh's daughter and Jesus escaped with His parents to Egypt, but what about all the babies who died? They were Jewish infants, Abraham's seed. How could God do this?

If we look at these scenarios with the understanding that all those infants went to heaven and got to be with God immediately rather than having to live difficult lives first, we see that they were greatly blessed.

Third, condemnation to hell is always linked to a list of abominations that a person commits. In His grace, God takes some infants before they can develop such a list: "And the dead were judged by what was written in the books, according to what they had done" (Rev. 20:12b). Men are saved by grace, but they are damned by works. What works have babies done?

In John 8:24, Jesus says, "I told you that you would die in your sins, for unless you believe that I am he you will die in your sins." Unbelief is the primary damning sin. Babies do not have the opportunity to express unbelief, so they are not able to commit this "unforgivable sin."

Babies are not innocent of the imputed sin of Adam, but they are innocent of personal sin because they have not had the opportunity to personally rebel against God. A number of thought-provoking verses support this assertion.

God said to Jonah, "And should not I pity Nineveh, that great city, in which there are more than 120,000 persons who do not know their right hand from their left?" (Jonah 4:11). In his excellent sermon series titled "What

Happens to Babies Who Die?" Dr. John MacArthur asserts that these people who did not know their right hands from their left hands must have been children. These children were part of the reason God wanted to save Nineveh. God said they deserved His compassion.

When Moses was about to die, he recounted God telling the Israelites who would enter the Promised Land: "And as for your little ones, who you said would become a prey, and your children, who today have no knowledge of good or evil, they shall go in there. And to them I will give it, and they shall possess it" (Deut. 1:39). God said that the children of the rebellious Israelites had no knowledge of good and evil.

God commanded Jeremiah to prophesy these words to the kings of Judah and the people of Jerusalem: "The people have forsaken me and have profaned this place by making offerings in it to other gods whom neither they nor their fathers nor the kings of Judah have known; and . . . they have filled this place with the blood of innocents" (Jer. 19:4). Idolatrous Israelites had sacrificed their children to other gods, but the children were not culpable—God called them "innocents."

Paul writes, "His invisible attributes, namely, his eternal power and divine nature, have been clearly perceived, ever since the creation of the world, in the things that have been made. So they are without excuse" (Rom. 1:20). This statement is not true of infants. They have not seen and perceived, and because of that, in some ways, they are "*with* excuse."

Fourth, in the New Testament, we find verses that speak of God's salvation of individuals from all "people groups" that have ever lived. For instance, Revelation 5:9 records a heavenly song of praise to Christ: "Worthy are you to take the scroll and to open its seals, for you were slain, and by your blood you ransomed people for God from every tribe and language and people and nation."

If we assume there have been people groups that have died out without ever hearing about Christ, how can every "tribe" be represented in heaven? This is possible only if children from those tribes died and were saved by the special grace of God. This understanding makes this verse much easier to comprehend and allows for a much more practical view of the end times.

Mature Understanding

Up to this point, we have been discussing the deaths of infants. But when does a child become an adult and take on responsibility for his eternal destination? What about unborn children who die—including those who are aborted—and mentally retarded or impaired individuals?

MacArthur addresses the point at which people cease to be children in God's eyes. He says it occurs when a person reaches "sufficient mature understanding to comprehend convincingly the issues of law, grace, sin, and salvation."[4]

This condition is not achieved at a specific age. Every child develops at a different rate and reaches the "mature understanding" at a different time in his or her life. Some may mature to this level at eight while others need until eighteen. Until the young person meets the requirements of biblical understanding, he is considered a "child" by God.

Since this is the case, it is clear that unborn babies, including those who are aborted, cannot possibly be accountable for their actions and are thus saved through the grace of God. This means that a believing woman who had an abortion in her youth can rest assured that her baby is in the hands of her loving Father in heaven. While she committed the sin of murder, her child was saved by God's grace, and grace can also be the means of her forgiveness.

The idea of "mature understanding" also helps us comprehend the fate of mentally retarded or impaired people. These individuals lack the means to express faith. God, therefore, regards them in the same way He looks at infants and saves them by His grace. This is a great comfort to parents who spend their entire lives caring for mentally handicapped children. The assurance that they will spend eternity in the new heaven and the new earth with their perfected children is a fabulous blessing of God.

It is possible that up to half of the world's population throughout history has died prior to reaching this mature understanding, and millions of babies (unborn and born) continue to die in this world every year. These babies are populating either heaven or hell at an incredible rate. I trust that it is heaven that is experiencing the "baby boom."

Therefore, we should not be spending our time here on earth worrying about our children who have died in infancy. They are in heaven with the Lord Jesus. Rather, we should be praying for our children who are old enough to exercise saving faith in Christ and resting in the comfort of knowing that we believe in a loving heavenly Father.

NOTES
1 R. C. Sproul, *Now, That's a Good Question!* (Wheaton, Ill.: Tyndale House, 1996), 294.

2 Charles H. Spurgeon, "Exposition of the Doctrines of Grace," *Spurgeon's Sermons*, Vol. 7, quoted in John MacArthur sermon series, "What Happens to Babies Who Die?" (Panorama City, Calif.: Grace to You Ministries, 2001).

3 B. B. Warfield, as quoted in MacArthur, "What Happens to Babies Who Die?"

4 MacArthur, "What Happens to Babies Who Die?"

WHAT TIES ALL THIS TOGETHER?

Man Asks, God Answers is designed to be an incentive for thought and a comfort for the faithful. It is meant to be an encouragement to Christians and seekers to think through what they believe about these issues and attempt to come to God-honoring conclusions about them.

Man is an inquisitive being. We are born with the ability to reason and wonder about who we are and why we are here. We have questions, but God gives us the answers if we are willing to look in the right places—and trust the answers He gives to us.

If you are a seeker struggling to find "truth," do not stop now. After reading this book, you need to read the

Bible, find a good, Bible-believing church in which to worship God, and read other Christian books. I have included a list of exceptional titles on the following page.

If there is one overriding theme to this book, it is the majesty of God. We want to put everything into a nice, neat package that we can understand. But that is not possible. We are not God. We are creatures and He is the Creator. We cannot begin to fathom how great and awesome our God is. Considering that He can and does do things that our minds believe to be contradictory helps us see how small our capacity for comprehension really is.

The God of this book is the only God I want to believe in. I do not want to have to worry about making the right decisions that will acquire for me the blessing of eternal life. Rather, I want a God who knows everything, has chosen me to live forever with Him, and will allow me to live this life on earth under His providence and blessings.

God is far greater than we understand Him to be. Hopefully, this book has opened your mind to an appreciation for what God has done for you and the great blessings that He has in store for His people.

"For my thoughts are not your thoughts, neither are your ways my ways, declares the LORD. For as the heavens are higher than the earth, so are my ways higher than your ways and my thoughts than your thoughts." (Isa 55:8–9)

Now to him who is able to do far more abundantly than all that we ask or think, according to the power at work within us, to him be glory in the church and in Christ Jesus throughout all generations, for ever and ever. Amen. (Eph. 3:20–21)

For Further Reading ↓

Louis Berkhof	*Systematic Theology*
	Manual of Christian Doctrine
John Blanchard	*Ultimate Questions*
	Where Do We Go From Here?
Loraine Boettner	*The Reformed Doctrine of Predestination*
James M. Boice	*The Doctrines of Grace: Rediscovering the Evangelical Gospel* (with Philip Graham Ryken)
	Foundations of the Christian Faith
	Whatever Happened to the Gospel of Grace? Rediscovering the Doctrines that Shook the World
John Calvin	*The Golden Booklet of the True Christian Life*
	Truth for All Time (A Brief Outline of the Christian Faith)
	Institutes of the Christian Religion
Gordon Clark	*What Do Presbyterians Believe?*
Leonard J. Coppes	*Are Five Points Enough? The Ten Points of Calvinism*

B. K. Kuiper   *The Church in History*
Steven J. Lawson   *Foundations of Grace*
John MacArthur   *Alone with God*
                        Hard to Believe
J. I. Packer   *Knowing God*
Arthur W. Pink   *The Sovereignty of God*
John Piper   *The Justification of God*
R. C. Sproul   *Essential Truths of the Christian Faith*
                        Reason to Believe
                        Chosen by God
                        What Is Reformed Theology?
                        Now, That's a Good Question!
David N. Steele   *The Five Points of Calvinism:*
                           Defined, Defended, Documented
                           (with Curtis C. Thomas and
                           S. Lance Quinn)
Johannes G. Vos   *The Westminster Larger Catechism:*
                           A Commentary

About the Author ↓

Craig Brown graduated from Geneva College, a Reformed Presbyterian (RP) school, with a degree in business administration in 1978. He is the president and CEO of Renaissance Nutrition, Inc., a firm that manufactures and markets nutritional products and services to dairy farmers throughout the United States and Canada.

He has served as a ruling elder in both the Orthodox Presbyterian Church and the Presbyterian Church in America.

Craig has been married to his wife, Rebecca, for more than 36 years and is the proud father of Heather, Christopher, and Victoria.